THE SUCCESSFUL CAREER SURVIVAL GUIDE

Praise for The Successful Career Survival Guide. . .

"This book is a difference maker for anyone at any stage of their career. Your perspective on employment, career, values, leadership, and the impact you will make every day will be influenced and revitalized by reading this critical survival guide."
Timothy C. Stansfield, PE, PhD, President, IET, Inc.

"This book is a collection of powerful career lessons and another wonderful addition to a great body of work created by Dr. Clint Longenecker. Clint's keen insight and experience will provide valuable learnings to the newly minted manager as well as the most seasoned professional. I give this book my highest endorsement."
David Wolf, President, Perstorp Polyols, Inc.

"Timeless truths deserve to be shared and can make a huge impact on receptive thinkers who care to be transformative. Clint's Successful Career Survival Guide *is a gift to every lifelong learner."*
Chuck Stocking, CEO, Principle Industries Inc.

"This book represents a well-organized and thought-out approach to dealing with some of the biggest challenges we face in managing and leading our careers: time management, relationships, planning, staying focused, and communicating effectively with others. Clint has a true passion for helping people achieve professional excellence and motivating them to be the best. His career-success thinking and lessons are things that you want to build into your team."
David L. Bishop, President & CEO, Matrix Technologies Inc.

"After reading The Successful Career Survival Guide *I came away truly excited and pumped up! This collection of career advice is spot-on and really hits home for me and our entire leadership team here at Endevis. As a business owner in a very high-performance industry, it is a challenge to get people on the same page, focused, and ready to perform day in and day out to deliver better results. This book is a valuable tool for each of our employees' development program and should be part of your organization's library as well! The lessons are invaluable!"*
Mark E. Melfi, CPC, Senior Managing Partner, Endevis

*"*The Successful Career Survival Guide *offers great advice and tools for self-improvement, both professionally and with life outside of work. The lessons that Clint shares are easy to understand and his road map for achieving personal transformation is clear. This book is a must-read for anyone hoping to compete in an increasingly competitive world."*
Chris Beach, CEO, The Bostwick-Braun Company

"This book does a great job of providing high powered, concise, and accurate information on career success. Readers will find that this book will not only improve their leadership abilities and organizational performance, but will serve as a great reference resource for many years to come. So keep this book handy!"
Chad Bringman, Executive Director, The Ronald McDonald House Charities NWO

*"*The Successful Career Survival Guide *is a wonderful collection of great business lessons and best practices for everyone who wants to advance their career and be the best person, professional, and leader that they can be. Clint has had a career of transforming people's lives and this book provides real insight on his success!"*
John Caponigro, Esq., CEO, Sports Management Network, Inc.

"This book is Life's Little Instruction Book *for the workplace. The message is simple but sure to be enjoyed by everyone. We know how important it is to be considerate and courageous, responsible and respectful. Sometimes though, life gets in the way, so it's nice to get a reminder. With this read, you gain a practical guidebook filled with key research findings, best practices, and direct observations to help people not only think but also to provide encouragement and ideas to find their way to success. Even if you already know how to live a purposeful life, you're going to gain reminders for serious personal development along with memorable quotes and ideas from some powerful leaders."*
Sheri Caldwell, PhD, SHRM-SCP, SPHR, HR Director for The Andersons, Inc. Grain Group

"If you want some great ideas on how to get better results, be more effective in your workplace, and improve your career opportunities, this is a book that you will truly use and appreciate!"
Mike Miller, CEO, Waterford Bank

"Clint delivers again with The Successful Career Survival Guide. *In this day of marketplace uncertainty this handbook is a must. One can pick it up at any time, turn to any page, and find a helpful nugget which could be the difference between sinking and swimming in their career."*
Jim Lange, President, 5feet20.com and author of *Calming the Storm Within: How to Find Peace in this Chaotic World*

"This book contains some invaluable lessons for every working professional who is serious about improving their performance, careers, and lives. I want to encourage you to take the time to learn these lessons so you are in a better position to make a bigger difference with your career."
Pete Davis, President, Dundee Manufacturing

Also by Clinton O. Longenecker

Getting Results: Five Absolutes for High Performance
with Jack Simonetti

The Two-Minute Drill: Lessons for Rapid Organizational Improvement from America's Greatest Game
with Gregg Papp and Tim Stansfield

The Great Courses: Critical Business Skills for Success
DVD Series and Course Guide

THE SUCCESSFUL CAREER SURVIVAL GUIDE

Clinton O. Longenecker Ph.D.

ISBN-13: 978-1544268750
ISBN-10: 1544268750

This book is dedicated to the best person I know on God's good earth, my lovely wife, Cindy. Thank you for being my everything—a great friend, soulmate, mother, teacher, counselor, helpmate, fellow traveler, and eternal love of my life!

You are simply THE BEST for me!

FOREWORD

In 1991 H. Jackson Brown wrote a best-selling book entitled *Life's Little Instruction Book,* which was a collection of 511 suggestions, observations, and reminders on how to live a happy and rewarding life. His book was a terrific assembly of important and practical things that each of us could and should do to experience greater satisfaction, joy, and fulfillment in our travels through life based on his personal life journey. He reminded his readers that they needed to "Take time to smell the roses," "Keep a tight rein on your temper," "VOTE," and "Compliment three people every day." And he went on to say, "Have impeccable manners," "Remember other people's birthdays," "Be kinder than necessary," and "Avoid negative people," among other pieces of great advice.

When I read the 511 axioms in this book I found it to be a wonderful reminder and a great checklist of things that could make my life better at many levels when properly implemented on a daily basis. And I found, more often than not, Mr. Jackson's counsel was spot-on. His thoughts made a great deal of sense to me and it's easy to see why his book was a best seller and created a new genre of simple, pointed self-help books.

Back in the day I asked myself, "What if there was a *Life's Little Instruction Book* for the workplace?" So several years ago I started assembling key findings from my ongoing business research projects on high-performance people and organizations, best practices from highly effective leaders that I have worked with over the years, and inspirational quotes, as well as business tips and lessons from a wide variety of interesting and highly successful people. Collectively, these resources are the backbone of this endeavor to create a guidebook or survival guide for the modern workplace.

The counsel offered in this book, when properly implemented, will help *you* be more effective and satisfied at work, have a greater talent for delivering desired results and making a difference at your place of employment, and give you a greater capacity to be more successful with your career and life. I am very thankful and appreciative for the opportunity to share with you what I have learned during my work-life journey, and I want to thank you for taking the time to invest in yourself by reading this book. THINK BIGGER!

Clinton O. Longenecker
Toledo, Ohio - 2017

PROLOGUE
Big Career Trouble!

Several years ago I was in my office trying to "dig out" from under a pretty substantial pile of emails, paperwork, and reports after being gone for several days on a business trip. I got a phone call out of the blue from a senior business leader whom I had met briefly at a speaking engagement with his organization several years earlier. His voice was tense when he asked me, "Clint, do you have time to talk for a couple minutes? I need some insight and I'm kind of struggling right now." Well, I learned a long time ago that when people are struggling and reach out, for whatever reason, it is critically important to give them your undivided attention when humanly possible. "Go on, Pat, it's good to hear from you. So tell me what's going on."

His somewhat urgent phone call had been brought on by an exceptionally disappointing meeting that he'd had earlier that day with his boss, the division president of a large service organization. In that meeting, the president had expressed his extreme disappointment in this leader's development and his inability to improve the performance of his operation after eighteen months on the job. And while Pat knew that things were not moving ahead as quickly as he would've liked, he didn't realize that things were so bad. He also had realized that his boss had now lost a certain level of faith in his ability to "move the performance needle in the right direction." This serious conversation with his boss had really shaken him to his core and caused him to reach out to me as a person he viewed as "an objective third-party."

Up to this point of his career, this leader had been exceptionally successful and he had rapidly climbed a very impressive career ladder. But now, for the first time in a long time, he wasn't sure what to do—but he was under tremendous pressure to do *something* to get back on track. He was quick to admit that he'd had ups and downs during his career like everyone else. But he was also quick to boast that he'd never had a business challenge or problem that he couldn't work his way out of! But all of a sudden Pat was feeling big pressure on multiple fronts in his life. He was putting in long hours at work, and trying to be a good husband and caring father, keep up with his responsibilities at home and in the community, stay in shape, and still be engaged with his extended family. At that moment, he wasn't sure what to do to improve his performance, and the frustration in his voice was palpable.

His meeting with the president that morning had hit him pretty hard and he was feeling defeated, disappointed, tired, frustrated, and overwhelmed. Pat was looking for someone to help him sort through where he was and help him develop a personal-improvement plan—in his words "to get back on track."

As we spoke, Pat made a very honest admission to me, one that most of us express at some point in our busy lives. "Clint, I feel like I am moving at a hundred miles an hour. I always have more on my plate than I can actually get done. I am in meetings all the time and when I'm there I'm thinking about all the things I should be doing. I feel like I am always caught up in minutia and that I am not spending my time and energy on the important things at work! I feel like I am shortchanging my family these days and I feel awful about it. And to make matters worse, I am tired all the time because I have a hard time sleeping at night because I have so many things on my mind. I am really frustrated right now and I don't know what to do, but I've got to do something right now."

I told Pat that I really appreciated his reaching out, his candor, and his willingness to share his frustrations with me on a very personal level. And I told him-I get phone calls and have conversations just like this with leaders and professionals in every walk of life pretty regularly. He certainly was not alone. All of us can have days where we feel just like Pat did, and given the pace of life these days, it doesn't take long to feel we've reached our capacity! The truly important thing was that he was *willing to take action* and that he realized that he couldn't keep doing what he'd been doing if things were going to change for the better.

After hearing this, Pat asked second time, "Clint, what do you think I should do?"

So I asked Pat, "When was the last time you took a **big step back** from the 'hamster wheel' to take a long, hard look at yourself and ask what you are really trying to accomplish with your life and career?"

His response was quick and honest: "**It has been a really long time; too long, I guess. But I have just been so busy. . . but I've got to figure out what I'm going to do now! I don't want to fail again and I need to get back on track!**"

Pat's response to my question was very typical. We are all so busy these days that it is easy to get "out of sync" with our true priorities. But in the end, Pat was admitting that he was human like the rest of us and that he allowed his work and life to spin out of

3

control. He had reached a point where his performance at work had hit a wall, his frustration with himself was high, and the fast pace of life had sucked dry his joy for life. (Can you relate to Pat's predicament?)

In these fast-paced, turbulent, and rapidly changing times, career success and survival is ultimately driven by a person's ability to *take control* of the things they can and must control. Each of us needs a plan to help us take control of the things that drive our professional and personal success!

Then I gave Pat the same advice that I offer to other leaders and professionals who come to me when they find themselves struggling with their careers: Before we meet together, take a "personal strategic planning retreat" with yourself. Go to a park or find a quiet place at the public library where you can sit and think and not be disturbed. Leave your phone behind, take a pad of paper and a pen, and a paper calendar. I need you to "unplug" for a couple hours so you can actually THINK! I am going to give you a list of twelve critically important questions that you need to answer for yourself in preparation for our discussion, and you need to give each question some serious thought because your answers are going to be vital in developing your personal improvement plan. Think of this as a "needs assessment" on yourself. You need to determine where you're at right now on some very important issues that can powerfully impact your success. When you do this you will be in a better position to figure out what you need to do to close the gap between where you are right now and where you want to be as a person and professional.

Pat responded with enthusiasm. "I like the idea and I already have a metropark in mind where I know I can go to hide out early

Saturday morning…I'm curious about these twelve questions. What are the questions? What do you want to know? Where did they come from? When can you get them to me?"

I told Pat that the questions I would send him are based on three decades of research and practice with thousands of high-performance professionals from virtually every industry in America. I reminded him to give each question serious thought, and we concluded our 45-minute phone call.

As Pat was hanging up he said, "Thanks again, Clint, for your time. I feel better for getting all this stuff off my chest. I want you to know that I'm taking this assignment very seriously and I'll see you next Tuesday after work. And don't forget to send those questions, okay?"

INTRODUCTION
Career Success and Survival in the 21st Century

I chose to open this book with this account of Pat because most of us can relate to him and his current dilemma in one way or another. At the completion of this book, I'll tell you what he learned at his "day at the park" and how things turned out for Pat.

Now most of us who are professionals and leaders like Pat are exceptionally busy, and living in the "information age" has exacerbated the complexity and pace of our already busy lives. You see, the average American professional spends nearly 2400 hours at work each year, and while many people truly enjoy their work, a disproportionate number of people do not. That same American worker will have on average nearly 12 different jobs over the course of their 45-year working career, will work for at least 6 different organizations, and will retire at around 67 years of age.

While the numbers show we spend only 28 percent of our consumable time each week at work, that percentage doesn't include time needed to get ready for work, the commute back and forth, and the work that so frequently rides home with us. And these days, most of us also bring home our considerable "work backpacks" filled with a variety of intellectual, emotional, and even political items that can sure make it seem like we can never get away from work. And let's be honest, it can really be draining and disheartening—that's what Pat was experiencing in a major-league way. Can you relate?

Now if your work backpack is like mine, it typically contains a lot of both tangible and intangible things like paperwork, reports, lots of emails, numerous text messages, phone calls, and time sensitive projects as well as always being "available." But that same work backpack can also contain a lot of work-related stress, concerns, frustrations, drama, second-guessing, and a tangle of apprehensions about keeping our jobs, doing the right thing, and advancing our careers!

I don't know about you, but I see a lot of people carrying around some pretty big work backpacks these days when they are supposed to be away from work, enjoying their families and personal time, and having "a life" outside of work.

And while our jobs can be all-encompassing and physically, emotionally, and intellectually draining at times, getting up each day and going to work is typically a non-negotiable part of the human condition. We all need to work to earn a living. But at the same time we need to have a sense of purpose, meaning, and accomplishment in our lives. I say this because it is one of my core beliefs that most people truly want to be successful in their endeavors at work, feel as if they are making a difference each day, and want to believe that they are advancing their careers and station in life by their daily pursuits!

Our quest for success can come in many shapes and forms but here are some critically important things we need to consider. I truly believe, and a lot of research would back me up on this, that we all want a number of things from work that go well beyond titles, accolades, and the size of our paychecks. We all want a daily sense of purpose and a workplace that allows us to get things done. We all want to go home at the end of each week with a sense of achievement and closure around the things that we set out to accomplish. We all want a monthly sense of triumph and self-actualization so we can look back and say, "It was a really good month," or "I got a lot done!" or "I really made a difference." And we all want an annual sense that we made progress in our work lives and that we have advanced our careers and improved our livelihoods! Having said this, I believe that most people want to do a good job for their employers and that they are willing to work hard to do so! I also believe that we all bring our values, passion, talents, and aspirations to work every day. Yet, we know that the modern workplace can, at times, be a very challenging, frustrating, impersonal, political, and stressful place to be.

I have been an avid student of understanding work and organizational life for well over three decades—truly hard to believe, but our careers go by so very quickly! So as your tour guide through this book, here's a little bit about my work-life journey. I grew up in a family-owned construction firm that struggled and went out of business before it got to the third generation. I have had the privilege of working in and consulting with an exceptionally wide variety of organizations from the shop floor to the C suite, from Wall Street to Main Street, and lots of organizations in between. I have spent time in both the public and private sector and I've had the privilege of leading a wide variety of large-scale organizational improvement and transformation programs and projects. I've also had the honor of working closely with some of the best senior leaders in the United States Armed Forces here and abroad and have learned many lessons in the process!

As a business educator and transformer, I have conducted executive/leadership development and training programs with thousands of professionals and leaders around the globe and have researched and written extensively about a wide variety of important business topics. I have studied leader and organizational success and failure, human performance in the workplace, effective coaching and teambuilding, how to create high-performance business enterprises, the power and importance of mentoring, and rapid organizational change. And I truly feel very fortunate to be a lifelong learner who has had the opportunity to do a lot of different things in a lot of truly impressive organizations where I have learned a great deal!

But of all the things that I have learned during my lifetime of working in and studying organizations, the one topic that has always been closest to my heart is that of **career success and survival.** I was introduced to this topic in the late 1980s by one of my colleagues and mentors, Dr. Jack Simonetti, when we conducted some original research to identify the factors that significantly impact and drive people's success in the workplace. Participants were asked to identify the factors that they considered to be most critical for their career success and survival. The findings were very interesting and became the basis for a wide variety of leadership- and management-development programs to help better equip people for success.

Since then I have conducted multiple research projects on this topic and most recently have sought out the input of over ten thousand high-performance professionals. The findings of this most recent study have been distilled into what I have come to call the **Career Success and Survival Imperatives** for the twenty-first century. It is vital to know and understand each of these 12 goals *before* we jump into the 707 pieces of advice for the same reason we ought to know our destination before we get in the car. Each one of these imperatives represents a critical component for keeping your career moving in the right direction. These directives must be known, understood, applied, and mastered if a person is serious about being a high performer and taking their career to the next level!

These imperatives are very straightforward and logical when we calmly read them on the pages of a business article or book. But when we find ourselves immersed in the fast-paced, dynamic, and complex organizational structures of the twenty-first century, these important principles are often cast aside, forgotten, ignored, or even go unheeded in the heat of battle. So, before we begin our exploration and review of these imperatives please sit down at your laptop or get out your iPad or a piece of paper and clear your head. Now please answer the following question for yourself (the same question that we asked those who have participated in our research):

Based on your experience, what do you believe are the most important factors for keeping your career on track and moving in the right direction?

Take the time necessary to really think through this question and please be specific in writing out your detailed response. Once you are finished, please continue reading.

[I know you might be tempted to just read on without answering these questions, but please do your homework assignment first-please trust me on this one.]

The 12 Career Success and Survival Imperatives

I am going to predict that many of the things that you have written down are going to be rather similar to the findings that emerged from our research, so get out your list and compare our research findings on career success and survival with yours. The following are the **12 Career Success and Survival Imperatives** that have emerged from our extensive research, parsed out under four important headings that represent challenges that each and every working person must deal with if they are to keep their careers moving in the right direction. Each of these imperatives captures the specific actions that people in every organization, at every level, must consistently do to deliver higher levels of performance that can greatly improve a person's career trajectory. So let's review these challenges and key findings and see what we might learn.

CHALLENGE #1: ONGOING FOCUS AND ALIGNMENT - In the modern workplace, being busy does not equal being effective or successful! It is incumbent that every business professional creates focus around doing the right things, engages in daily activities that deliver desired outcomes, and makes the best use of their critical and scarce organizational resources! Having said this, here are our first three Career Success and Survival Imperatives:

1) **You must identify and deliver the value-added <u>results</u> your organization wants and needs from you and create a track record of doing so!**

2) **You must have the ability to recognize, implement, and master the key value-added <u>practices/behaviors</u> that lead to achieving these desired results.**

3) You must have the ability to focus your <u>time</u>, <u>organizational resources</u>, and <u>power</u> on delivering desired results.

CHALLENGE #2: CREATING REAL PEOPLE POWER - In the modern workplace it is exceptionally important to effectively interact with the people around us, whether they are superiors, peers, subordinates, customers, or organizational stakeholders. We must have the emotional intelligence and ability to work with everyone! The next three Career Success and Survival Imperatives make that perfectly clear:

4) You must place a high priority on forging and nurturing viable, meaningful, and effective <u>working relationships</u> and <u>networks</u>.

5) You must have the ability to effectively <u>communicate</u> and <u>connect with</u> everyone, in every situation.

6) You must maintain and project a positive <u>personality</u>, <u>attitude</u>, and <u>outlook</u> about yourself, your work, and your life.

CHALLENGE #3: ONGOING LEARNING AND PERFORMANCE IMPROVEMENT - Successful people must know how to create and maintain proper focus and build great working relationships with the people where they live and work. But it is critically important that they pay careful attention to the things going on around them and that they continually monitor and track their own performance. In addition, they must continuously learn and develop their skills, seek out ongoing feedback and coaching, and develop the ability to continuously solve problems and serve as change agents to help drive improvement in their enterprises. Thus, the following four Career Success and Survival Imperatives:

7) You must work hard to develop your "situational awareness" so you always know <u>what is going on</u> around you and <u>how well</u> you are actually performing.

8) You must continually <u>learn</u> and <u>develop yourself</u> with the <u>skills/talents</u> necessary to meet the changing demands of your job.

9) You must embrace honest <u>feedback</u> and <u>coaching</u> and seek out real <u>accountability</u>.

10) You must be a disciplined <u>problem-solver</u> and <u>change agent</u> who continuously looks for ways to make it easier to get things done!

CHALLENGE #4: TRUE GRIT PROFESSIONALISM AND CHARACTER - If a person practices the previous ten imperatives, I can state with great confidence that their performance will improve! But the last two Career Success and Survival Imperatives just might be the key to long-term success in workplace and life satisfaction. It is imperative that we all learn how to handle the things that life throws at us and that we continuously work hard to maintain our character and integrity. Our final two Career Imperatives include:

11) You must possess the ability to <u>handle stress</u>, <u>stay poised</u>, and <u>maintain balance</u> in every area of your personal and professional life.

12) You must demonstrate <u>character</u> and <u>integrity</u> in everything you do!

These Career Success and Survival Imperatives represent an "umbrella" for your thinking about what you can and must do to increase your performance at work to fully maximize your career potential! And we have discovered through our leadership research, development programs, and consulting initiatives that these

14

imperatives require a specific mindset and behaviors that can be developed, nurtured, and mastered when people are serious about being the best that they can be—and that is what this book is all about!

Career Success and Survival Assessment

To maximize your benefit from the contents of this book, start by doing a quick assessment of yourself and see how you stack up against these critically important performance drivers. You see, the ultimate factor that will determine your career success will be your ability to deliver high performance and desired results consistently with and through people, and mastering these imperatives will help you do just that.

The purpose of this assessment is to give you a baseline so you can effectively target your improvement efforts. As you assess yourself against each of these questions, please be honest with yourself to determine where you really stand. And while all of these questions do not carry equal weight in the career-success equation, they are all nonetheless important in generating high performance and career success. You will also be given the opportunity to repeat this assessment a second time at the end of this book to see if your thinking has changed or expanded.

Carefully read each question and rate yourself using the following scale to determine where you stand on each imperative:

1 = I am clearly failing at this imperative
2 = I am really struggling with this imperative
3 = I am barely adequate with this imperative
4 = I am good with this imperative
5 = I am exceptional with this imperative

1) I consistently identify and deliver the value-added <u>desired results</u> my organization wants and needs from me on an ongoing basis._____

2) I recognize, implement, and stay focused on the key value-added <u>practices/behaviors</u> that lead to desired results on an ongoing basis. _____

3) I focus my <u>time</u>, <u>organizational resources,</u> and <u>power</u> on delivering desired results. _____

4) I forge and foster viable, effective <u>working relationships</u> and <u>business networks</u> with the people I need to get desired results. _____

5) I effectively <u>communicate</u> and <u>connect with</u> everyone in every situation at work. _____

6) I work to maintain and project a positive <u>personality</u>, <u>attitude</u>, and <u>outlook</u> about myself, my work, and life. _____

7) I maintain my "<u>situational awareness</u>" so that I always <u>know what is going on</u> around me and <u>how well</u> I am actually performing. _____

8) I continually <u>learn</u> and <u>develop</u> the <u>skills/talents</u> necessary to meet the changing demands of my job. _____

9) I embrace <u>feedback</u> and <u>coaching</u> and seek out <u>accountability</u> for improvement. _____

10) I work hard to be a disciplined <u>problem-solver</u> and <u>change agent</u> to make it easier to get things done. _____

11) I effectively <u>handle stress</u>, <u>stay poised</u>, and <u>maintain balance</u> in every area of my personal and professional life. _____

12) I demonstrate <u>character</u> and <u>integrity</u> in all of my personal and professional dealings. _____

SCORING: In the space provided below please write down your score for each of these 12 questions and fill out the subtotal for each section. When that is complete, add up your four subtotal scores and determine your **GRAND TOTAL.**

Ongoing Focus and Alignment

Question #1: _____

Question #2: _____

Question #3: _____

SUBTOTAL: _____

Creating Real People Power

Question #4: _____

Question #5: _____

Question #6: _____

SUBTOTAL: _____

Ongoing Learning and Performance Improvement

Question #7: _____

Question #8: _____

Question #9: _____

Question #10: _____

SUBTOTAL: _____

True Grit Professionalism and Character

Question #11: _____

Question #12: _____

SUBTOTAL: _____

GRAND TOTAL (all four sections): _____

The purpose of this 12-point questionnaire is to get you to think candidly about your performance on these critically important performance-enhancing practices that can have a powerful effect on your career trajectory. On some of these imperatives you might score quite high and for others you might need some serious work, but what is important now is that you are thinking about the impact that each of these imperatives can have on your ability to be successful and effective in your current position at work.

If you find yourself having a score of less than three on any of these 12 imperatives, stop and carefully think about how you are going to improve this area. Use the following scoring to determine where you stand based on your assessment of yourself. Remember the goal here is to get you to THINK!

Score 12–23: Career Danger Zone

Score 24–35: Career Success Improvement Required

Score 36–47: Career Strengths Are Emerging

Score 48–60: Career Strengths Are in Place

So how did you stack up against the 12 Career Success and Survival Imperatives? If you're like myself and most of the people that I work with, keeping in tune and up to speed in all 12 of these key performance drivers is an ongoing process!

And that is the purpose of this book-to dedicate time and space to providing you vision, ideas, best practices, inspiration, reminders, and common- sense thinking about how to improve in each of these overarching career imperatives.

For the past 30 years the goal of my research, teaching, leadership development, consulting, and executive coaching has been to help leaders and professionals in every discipline increase their personal effectiveness and success, and I've learned a lot along the way about how to get these principles to "stick." So to best absorb all the research and advice of this book, I strongly suggest you keep a **Career Imperative Note Sheet**; when an idea resonates with you, circle the number and keep a record on your laptop, iPad, phone, or piece of paper. As you read, do so with an eye on evaluation, integration, and application of these ideas to make the necessary changes needed for you to reach your full potential as a person and professional in each of the overarching performance categories: ***Ongoing Focus and Alignment, Creating Real People Power, Ongoing Learning and Performance Improvement,*** and ***True Grit Professionalism and Character.***

As you read and apply these practices and ideas to your life you will discover and be reminded that getting better performance and being successful comes down to practicing these fundamentals with passion, proficiency, and discipline. To do so will greatly enhance your life and career. And remember that we are all students in life with lots to learn regardless of our age, position, or station!

TIME TO THINK!
Ideas, Concepts, and Practices for Improving Your Mindset and Performance on the Career Success and Survival Imperatives!

ONGOING FOCUS AND ALIGNMENT

"Just as your car runs more smoothly and requires less energy to go faster and farther when the wheels are in perfect alignment, you perform better when your thoughts, feelings, emotions, goals, and values are in balance."

-Brian Tracy

1. Remember and live by this critically important fact: Getting desired results with and through people the right way and at the right time is the #1 factor for long-term career success in virtually every organization on the planet!

2. Regardless of your job, you must **always** perform "value-added work" that is clearly linked to your organization's mission, goals, priorities, overall performance, and profitability.

3. Take the time to define what success really means to you and do it in writing.

    Your definition for success will evolve, but you must articulate what you really want to accomplish with your career, and what you will stand for in doing so!

4. No matter what happens at work always **stay calm** and **carry on** by **focusing** on what you are being paid to accomplish! Losing this focus can lead to frustration, ineffectiveness, and, if left unchecked, failure.

5. Spending too much of your time and energy doing "non-value-added work" is to court termination, downsizing, and career disaster. Don't do it!

6. # Never mistake being busy with being productive!

7. REALITY CHECK: According to our research, on average less than 40 percent of employees are completely confident that they are on the same page with their boss in terms of their roles, goals, and responsibilities! How about you?

8. Work hard to build your career around the things you consider to be truly important. You need to invest your time and talent doing work in a position with an organization that will allow you to experience real job satisfaction!

9. "We are what we repeatedly do. Excellence, then, is not an act, but a habit." -Aristotle

10. It is critically important to know which behaviors, activities, and results are most considered by your organization for promotions.

11. It is equally important to know which behaviors, activities, and performance factors are most important in your organization for getting terminated, demoted, put out to pasture, or down-sized.

12. If you've occupied a position for more than two weeks and do not have clear marching orders and a job description from your boss, you must take action. Sit down and develop a written list of what you believe your job entails and schedule a meeting with your boss to get on the same page now!

13. Know your company's mission statement by heart. If you don't, get a copy and place it somewhere you can look at it regularly to better understand your purpose and context for doing the things you do!

14. There is almost always an <u>inverse</u> relationship between the length of an organization's mission statement and its likelihood of creating vision, inspiring, and driving action, so learn how to draw meaning from your organization's lengthy mission statement even if it is not obvious! Your organization's mission statement is just a group of words until your actions line up to support your organization's mission.

15. "It goes without saying that no company, small or large, can win over the long run without energized

employees who believe in the mission and understand how to achieve it." -Jack Welch

16. **Develop a PERSONAL mission statement that captures the following: what you are being paid to deliver, your core values, and your key operating principles that make you who you are. And go online and pull down some examples to help fuel your thinking.**

    (Oh and by the way, here's my Personal Mission Statement: To always inspire, help, equip, and transform others to succeed by doing the right things, the right way, at the right time!)

17. Always know and understand the factors that influence and drive your organization's ability to be profitable. Always know and understand the factors that influence and drive your organization's ability to grow market share, as well.

18. **Know and understand how to make sense out your organization's financial statements.**

19. You will increase your influence and career success in your organization when you can solve problems that impact your organization's revenues, cost structure, and customer satisfaction!

20. Take the time to make sure that you know exactly how your job impacts your organization's bottom line! This

is a good discussion to have with your boss so you can come away with some real specifics.

21.   At the same time, know and understand how your job affects the overall performance of your operating unit.

22.   During the course of one's career, Americans have on average 12 different jobs, with a range of 4 to 15 different jobs.

(See htpp://www.bis.gov/nisfags.htm#anch41)

Consider this: What causes people to move from one job to another, and when they do, are they doing it on their terms? Ask several of your friends to offer up their opinions and experiences and see what you might learn!

23.   Know that high performance on your part creates real career opportunities. Conversely, poor and mediocre performance closes career doors rather quickly.

24.   "Our plans miscarry because they have no aim. When a man does not know what harbor he is making for, no wind is the right wind." -Seneca

25.   Where there is ambiguity about your roles, goals, and responsibilities there is the absence of focus and an increase in uncertainty. Fact: A lack of focus and employee uncertainty will <u>always</u> damage human performance at work!

26.   To have a successful and meaningful career, it is critically important to know the difference between being ignorant, being stupid, and being wise!

27. At work, ignorance is never bliss! If you find yourself not knowing what to do, immediately take action to discover what you need to know to be successful. And do so sooner rather than later!

28. Don't do stupid stuff!

Stupidity is when a person knows the right thing to do but for whatever reason chooses not to do it. Know that if you are doing stupid things at work, these actions will eventually catch up with YOU with highly unpredictable consequences!

29. Long-term career success requires real wisdom, so learn and know what you need to do, and develop the motivation and discipline to do it well, both personally and professionally!

To not do so is to make life more difficult for yourself than it needs to be!

30. "The successful warrior is the average man, with laser-like focus." -Bruce Lee

31. Never go into battle unprepared—don't allow it to happen to either you or your team members because a lack of preparation always spells trouble, and sometimes even disaster!

32. Never forget the six biggest reasons we have learned for employee termination: poor performance, lack of necessary talent, an inability or unwillingness to improve, poor work ethic, having a bad attitude, and poor people skills!

33. Remember what Thoreau said, "This time, like all times, is a very good one, if we but know what to do with it." It is our job (and challenge) to figure out what to do with our gift of time!

34. Always know exactly what your internal and/or external customers need from you and set up a system to deliver. Measure your performance in this regard so you always know whether or not you are meeting and exceeding customer expectations on an ongoing basis!

35. Extensive research for the past five decades demonstrates a simple fact: People who have clear goals and focus outperform those who do not! This reality seems pretty obvious until we stop and realize that it is easy to find ourselves operating without goals and focus—if we're not careful. Never operate without knowing exactly what you need to accomplish!

36. Remember that goals not only create focus and a target to strive for, but they also set the stage for effective planning, time management, and resource

deployment, all of which are critical to goal attainment and success.

37. **"Always remember, your focus determines your reality." -George Lucas**

38. Know that it is critically important to get and stay on the same page with your boss and work closely with them to establish a clear link between your daily activities and deliverables and your boss's success.

39. Ask yourself and answer this question in a 500-word essay: What is my reputation at work as a person and performer? Be honest with yourself and see what you learn!

40. Take this exercise to the next level by asking three people at work (whom you trust) to write the same 500-word essay on you and see what you learn!

41. Work hard and carefully to develop a reputation as a person who solves problems and gets real work done in a timely fashion. Make this your "brand."

42. "You can't build a reputation on what you are going to do." -Henry Ford

43. REMEMBER: Time is your most important resource! **So learn how to treasure time and invest it ever so wisely!**

44. Be smart and strong enough to never allow meetings to consume a disproportionate amount of the time you have available to get real, results-oriented work accomplished.

45. Think of the worst three meetings that you have ever attended. Now make a list of what made them the worst and make a pledge to yourself that you will not fall prey to these bad behaviors/practices when <u>you</u> run meetings!

46. Read Patrick Lencioni's best-selling book, *Death by Meeting* to get some awesome ideas about how to deal with this potentially useful but often painful and wasteful organizational ritual called *meetings*!

47. Learn how to make good use of online tools such as GoToMeeting to bring people together quickly without the hassle, time, and costs of travel!

48. Master your talent for running focused, engaging, timely, and useful meetings. To not do so is to waste resources, demotivate and frustrate people, and damage your credibility as a leader.

49. Never start a meeting without declaring its purpose, clearly stating the desired outcomes, establishing ground rules, and sharing why this gathering is worth people's time! A clearly stated purpose for a meeting, when perfected, can help eliminate the organizational time-wasting "worthless meeting syndrome" that virtually everyone can fall prey to!

50. Know that long meetings at the start of any workday can quickly suck the energy out of people unless they are exceptionally crisp and well run!

51. Two great times for meetings are 11:30 a.m., before lunch, and 4:30 p.m., at the back end of the workday. You'll see a marked increase in focus, attention span

and willingness to take action when meeting in these timeslots!

52. To have more effective meetings, encourage "stand-up meetings," from time to time, with attendees standing around the conference room table—this can help people become more engaged and more focused! (At the same time, be sensitive to ADA issues.)

53. When a meeting is dragging on, going nowhere, drifting from the agenda, degenerating into countless side discussions, and summarily wasting valuable time, be brave enough to ask, *"What are we ultimately trying to get done here?"*

54. Start and stop all meetings on time as this practice will say a lot about you as a professional and as a leader. If a meeting is going long, ask participants for additional minutes and stick to the schedule so that they know you are being sensitive to their time.

55. ## Make it a personal practice to under-promise and over-deliver!

56. Know and understand how your organization's budgeting process works!

57. Become a student of Italian economist, engineer, sociologist, and philosopher Vilfredo Pareto who is credited with developing the 80/20 Rule.

   ✓ Identify the 20% of your activities that will deliver 80% of your desired outcomes. These are your "prime" activities.

✓ Once you've identified your 20% primary activities, carefully dedicate your time to these activities, and guard this time tenaciously!

58. This 80/20 identification process is critical to your career success and your ability to deliver desired results in every position you'll ever hold!

59. Take the time to identify the primary time wasters that are part of your personal and work life.

Our research continuously shows that constant interruptions, non-essential emails, unproductive meetings, workplace drama, broken processes, unresolved workplace conflicts, and poorly performing employees are the primary time wasters for most people!

60. As Plato's Socrates character said in *Phaedrus*, "Know thyself." I would add, "Know thyself when you become too busy!" Our research sample of over 2000 professionals clearly demonstrates that prolonged, extreme busyness degrades our ability to do the things that create value and deliver desired results for our organizations!

61. Never lose sight of what you are ultimately trying to achieve regardless of how busy you are.

62. Know and understand how being "too busy" negatively impacts your attention to detail, problem-solving skills, and ability to think clearly!

63. Know and understand how being "too busy" negatively impacts your interpersonal relationships, attitude, and ability to communicate effectively!

64. Know and truly understand how being "too busy" negatively impacts your stress levels, health, and sleep patterns!

65. Remember what Benjamin Franklin said about time: "Lost time is never found again." Remember this when you find yourself doing things at work and in life that waste your precious time!

66. Take time to develop a daily work plan to map out what needs to be accomplished so you can prioritize the use of your time, effort, and energy.

67. **Remember the Rule of 15/5/5:** Taking 15 minutes at the start of your day to plan and organize, 5 minutes midday to make adjustments, and 5 minutes at the end of the day for a postgame analysis simply makes sense, and it can have a profound effect on your ability to become focused and stay that way!

68. Key Point: 25 minutes of a 9-hour workday equals only 4.62% of the day. Our research has shown that this investment of time can deliver significant increases in personal productivity, improved working relationships, and a greater sense of workplace achievement when properly applied.

69. **Take 15 minutes at the start of every day to S.T.O.P.** — Sit-Think-Optimize-Perform.

In that time you can organize a plan for how you will invest your day to best deliver desired RESULTS! Use these 15 minutes to learn how to slow down, *sit,* and be still to allow your mind to unwind and get focused on the important things that you need to be thinking about and doing each day.

70.   Use your daily S.T.O.P. to *think* and to develop your "performance script" that you will use to *optimize* your performance each day and minimize wasting your time, talent, and treasure.

71.   While making lists can be psychologically rewarding (because it feels so good to scratch things off our list) they generally give the illusion of being organized. When identifying all the things that you wish to accomplish on a given day you must always thoughtfully prioritize your actions and activities and attach a conservative time estimate to each to see if you are setting yourself up for failure by putting more work on your plate than can be realistically accomplished!

72.   Take a time-out: Virtually every sport on earth uses a form of a "time-out" to assess where they are and make adjustments to perform at a higher level for the second half. Do the same for yourself at work—just five minutes at midday—on a daily basis!

73.   At the end of each day, take five minutes to write down what you learned, what was completed, and what didn't get done so you are ready to have your S.T.O.P. the next day. According to our research, this small percentage of time can have a significant impact on your personal effectiveness, satisfaction, and ability to deliver superior performance!

74.   Make sure that you schedule a percentage of your daily work time with yourself and hide if necessary to get

real results-oriented work done. Protect your productive work time and don't be AFRAID to let people know that you are not to be disturbed unless it is an emergency.

75. ## DO NOT waste other people's time. Learn how to be sensitive to other people in this regard!

76. To make better use of your resource of time, look for ways to minimize (or avoid altogether) drive and travel time without sacrificing the benefits that can come from face-to-face meetings.

77. Before you start on any new project or initiative, always define what winning will look like!

78. ## It has been said that failing to plan is planning to fail—so take sufficient time to plan on a regular basis to reduce the likelihood of unanticipated failure.

79. ## Use all the resources your organization has entrusted to you as if you paid for them yourself.

80. When you find yourself not being sure of how to respond in a stressful situation, remember Abraham Lincoln's words: "Better to remain silent and be thought a fool than to speak and remove all doubt."

81. ## Take time regularly to **THINK BIG**!

82. "Making good decisions is a crucial skill at every level of an organization." -Peter Drucker

83. Learn to solve problems and make good decisions FAST. Speed is critical these days to most organizational decisions and subsequent actions!

84. Always know what it takes to make your customers happy (whether internal or external) and take quick action when you don't.

85. Never start a project without clarifying the desired outcomes or deliverables that are needed for success.

86. Always know where your authority starts and stops so that you can make realistic and educated decisions.

87. Always take a mid-week "time-out" and stop to identify how you've spent your time to-date and determine what you've actually accomplished . . . if necessary, make adjustments and finish off the week strong and knowing you optimized your time!

88. Remember: The urgent is seldom important and the important is seldom urgent, so don't allow daily "firefighting" to get in the way of accomplishing the really important things that are necessary to your success.

89. Set SMART goals for yourself that reflect the outcomes you need to accomplish to keep your job and get ahead: Specific Measurable Achievable Results-based goals with a Time-table.

90. There is no substitute for hard work, sweat, persistence, and diligence in taking any project through to completion.

91. Set realistic and meaningful deadlines for the things that you are working on and develop a reputation for hitting them.

92. Work hard to balance your concern for the tasks that you need to accomplish with real concern for the people you work with.

93. Get in the habit of writing a trip report after all travel detailing your activity and accomplishments and share it with your boss.

94. Learn to look at the "big picture" for your current position to determine how it will help your career in the long run.

95. "Nothing limits achievement like small thinking. Nothing expands possibilities like unleashed thinking." -William Arthur Ward

96. Make it a real priority take control of your calendar as it has a powerful impact on your daily activity as well as your outlook on life!

97. Here is an important question for everyone:

What do you want your legacy to be at your place of employment?

The answer to this question should have a profound effect on how you do your work and interact with your co-workers on a daily basis!

98. Always make sure that you and your fellow team members know the WHY behind the WHAT you are being asked to do.

   When people cannot give you a satisfactory WHY behind the WHAT you are being asked to do, you will have a very difficult time achieving high performance!

99. When your boss delegates a new responsibility or a project to you, make sure that you clarify within your role...

   ... the deliverables that you are expected produce,

   ... the authority or sanction that you will need to operate,

   ... the resources that will be necessary for success,

   ... and the timeline for completion!

100. Never take on new responsibilities or projects without discussing and documenting these critical issues with your boss in detail!

101. If you are already extremely busy focusing on delivering the results attached to your job, seriously count the cost of taking on additional work or special assignments before saying yes! Overloading yourself can easily damage workplace performance and suck the joy out of life!

102. Remember it is hard to finish right when you start wrong! Take great care whenever you take on something new, whether it is a job assignment, project, or improvement initiative (and especially something outside of your current wheelhouse or comfort zone).

103. According to Gallup's Work and Education polls, the typical full-time adult worker in the US averages 47 hours of work per week! Based on your experience, what percentage of that workweek is productive and focused on delivering desired results?

Our research shows that the average professional has 2–3 hours per day for getting real, tangible, results-oriented work accomplished! What's wrong with this picture?

104. When you learn something about your competitors' strengths and weaknesses, blind spots, or *vulnerabilities*, share it with someone in your organization who is in a position to use this important information (and do so whether it is part of your job to do so or not)!

105. When writing reports, always be sure *why* you are doing it, *what* people are looking for in terms of content, and *how* the information will be used. Make sure this is a value-added activity.

106. When writing reports, remember that less is typically more and greatly appreciated! People love it when people know how to write effective, short, and cogent reports!

107. When you find yourself engaged in extremely time-consuming activity at work, make sure that you can always answer the question:

WHY AM I DOING THIS?

108. Be extremely careful about pursuing organizational growth if it doesn't satisfy your enterprise's minimum profitability goals. You just might find yourself being busier without any real corresponding benefits.

109. Remember a strategic plan is only useful when it actually influences the way in which people in your enterprise operate on a daily basis. Key question: Is your strategic plan making a real difference in your organization's daily operation? If not, why not?

110. Develop a schedule to contact your customers at a time they least expect it, just to see how they are doing, and to let them know that you truly care.

111. "We have two ears and one mouth so that we can listen twice as much as we speak." -Epictetus, a Greek philosopher

112. Learn to be busy without being in a rush.

113. Always know the primary reason your customers are YOUR customers. Is it your price, products, ability to solve their problems, or customer service?

114. Develop speed in handling the things that come across your desk and learn to quickly separate the

important things from clutter, distractions, and "organizational flotsam and jetsam."

115. When traveling on business, spend money like it is your own.

116. In 1962, Alfred DuPont Chandler, of the Harvard business school, wrote the business classic, *Strategy and Structure* in which he analyzed the behavior of the largest organizations in America at the time and how they handled change. This classic is still worth reading today to understand several important points on organizational and personal success! Chandler found:

   ✓ Businesses typically change only when they are forced to do so.
   ✓ Businesses must continuously monitor their environments and stakeholders if they are to remain relevant!
   ✓ Businesses must always be effective to succeed; that is, they must constantly adjust to their changing environment.
   ✓ Businesses must also be efficient—meaning they must consistently do things right!

   So here's a question for you: "What are the ramifications of these four key findings/principles to your effectiveness at work and your career success and survival?"

117. Your customers just might have your next new product or breakthrough idea. Are you close to your customer? Are you systematically listening to your customers on an ongoing basis? Do you regularly engage with them to help them solve problems? If not, why not?

118. Never confuse effective marketing with effective sales. Know the differences and the interdependency of each. Know also how these critically important functions apply to your career advancement in your enterprise!

119. Work to stay organized! Occasionally take the time to get "caught up" to ensure that you are operating in an optimal fashion. To not do so is to accept inefficiency, waste, and frustration!

120. If you struggle with procrastination, address the problem now, because in a fast-paced world, it can be a career killer. Suggestion: Move due dates forward, create accountability for deadlines, and develop better planning skills as a start. But do these things now!

121. Develop and use a planning model that is appropriate and effective for your current position and that forces you to think about the future and what needs to happen and when. Once this planning model has been established, *use it on a regular basis!*

122. Most people's workdays consist of less than 40 percent productive, results-oriented time. Find a way to gradually increase that number to 60 percent and you will be amazed how much work can actually be accomplished.

123. Don't waste time pursuing the goal of creating a "paperless" work environment because it won't

happen. The goal should be to create an *efficient* work environment, and leave it at that.

124. Whether you realize it or not you are a person of influence in your organization! You might have some influence or you might have tremendous influence, so remember:

125. High performance and success at getting things done will only increase your influence in your organization!

126. The more influence you have in your enterprise and industry, the easier it typically is to get things done and make a difference!

CREATING PEOPLE POWER

"I've learned that people will forget what you said, people will forget what you did, but people will never forget how you made them feel." -Maya Angelou

127. WORKPLACE FACT: People do not like to work with, be around, or communicate with people who are cynical, negative, malicious, mean, catty, angry, vicious, rancorous, unkind, spiteful, pessimistic, gloomy, glum, petty, or sarcastic.

NEVER allow these negative personality traits to creep into your work or personal life! And if you find yourself in possession of these traits, monitor

yourself and find a way to alleviate them systematically! To not do so ensures that people will not want to work with you and that your future will be limited!

128. "People won't have time for you if you are always angry or complaining." -Stephen Hawking

129. When working with people in close spaces, go easy on the cologne or perfume. An overwhelming scent can damage interpersonal relationships and teamwork as well as cause eyes to water!

130. If you want to be inspired and be reminded that one person can make a real difference, watch the Oscar-winning 1982 movie *Gandhi* directed by Sir Richard Attenborough. It will be absolutely worth your time and you will learn some great leadership lessons about perseverance and out-of-the-box thinking!

131. Always remember to look members of the US workforce in the eyes when you talk to them. However, be sensitive of this practice when operating in international or cross-cultural environments as not everyone around the world operates this way!

132. "If you want to go fast, go alone. If you want to go far, go together." -African proverb

133. Never underestimate the importance of asking, considering, and acting on the opinions of others.

134. Make it a personal priority to demonstrate uncommon courtesy to *all* your coworkers, from custodians to the CEO and everyone in between. Open the door for others, properly greet people, hold the elevator, ask

people who appear to be lost if you might assist them, and be friendly when you move around your place of employment. These courtesies are just the start of the countless ways you can develop a positive work environment.

135. Do not underestimate the power of having a great working relationship with your boss and its impact on your career success!

136. **Know that bad bosses are the #1 reason why employees choose to leave their current employer.** Accordingly, bad bosses cost their organizations huge dollars because of this unnecessary attrition and drama!

137. Put yourself in your boss's shoes: Make it a priority to know what results your boss is being paid to deliver so you are in a better position to help him or her be successful!

Be proactive and diligent in creating and maintaining this critical alignment so you and your boss can better operate in concert with each other!

138. Take the time to learn what you can about your boss's boss so you can understand what your boss is up against in trying to perform his/her job!

139. Accept the fact that you are not in a position to change your boss. One more time, and repeat after me: Accept the fact that you are not in a position to change your boss!

140. Carefully observe and study your boss to know and understand their strengths and weaknesses. Always know your boss's moods, habits, peculiarities, idiosyncrasies, and eccentricities so you will know how and when to best interact with him/her at any given point in time.

141. "The most important thing in communication is hearing what isn't said." -Peter Drucker

142. Regularly assess the quality of your current working relationship with your boss and conduct an annual SWOT analysis to determine the specific things that can be done to improve your relationship!

143. Take the initiative to regularly meet with your boss to keep them informed of what you're working on, progress, and priorities and to seek their input and guidance!

144. Be confident enough to ask your boss how they are doing and if there is anything that you can do to help them! Most employees are reluctant to do this with their superiors, but a small question like this goes a long way in communicating your dedication to *every* part of the team.

145. Never identify a problem or bring a complaint to your boss without providing a potential solution or plan of attack in writing.

146. Know that our bosses typically take things that are in writing more seriously than just word-of-mouth suggestions, ideas, complaints, or assessments.

147. Learn how to communicate using your boss's rules and interact with them on their terms!

148. Always show respect for your boss even if they don't deserve it! Take this spin on a well-known piece of advice: If you don't have something good to say about your boss, then it's probably best not to say anything!

149. **Never engage in gossip, backbiting, character assassination, or making your boss look bad in front of others.** Remember that bashing your boss reflects poorly on you and sets a terrible example for others in your enterprise, so don't do it.

150. When bosses learn that they are being disrespected behind their backs by their direct reports, careers of certain individuals can take an unexpected turn for the worse.

151. Use your judgment and wisdom to know when it is time to leave your current employer, such as when your boss …

- ✓ No longer cares about your development
- ✓ Freezes you out of the communications loop
- ✓ Makes coming to work a drag
- ✓ Keeps you from sleeping soundly
- ✓ Begins to impact your health and stress levels
- ✓ Is uncaring, narcissistic, egocentric, and megalo-maniacal
- ✓ Is dragging the entire department down

✓ Is engaged in unscrupulous, dubious, nefarious or illegal activities (In this case it just may be time to *run*!)
✓ Specifically tells you that you no longer have a future with the enterprise

152. When you have made your decision to leave your job because of your boss, immediately develop an exit strategy and time frame that you can rapidly execute.

153. Never let a bad boss permanently damage your health, performance, attitude, and belief in the human race!

154. Always be exceedingly careful and mindful about the conversations you choose to have in the restroom, elevator, cafeteria, or breakroom at work.

155. Do not allow yourself to become addicted to Facebook, LinkedIn, or other social media. The time expended generally outweighs any real return-on-investment for most working people!

156. Work hard to build truly effective, viable working relationships with the people you need to get your work done.

157. Remember more people are fired from their jobs because of poor people skills than any other reason!

Because of this fact you have every incentive to develop your "emotional intelligence" and interpersonal skills!

158. Take the time to actually proofread your emails as they speak volumes about your attention to detail.

159. *"The challenge of leadership is to be strong, but not rude; be kind, but not weak; be bold, but not bully; be thoughtful, but not lazy; be humble, but not timid; be proud, but not arrogant; have humor, but without folly." -Jim Rohn*

There are lots of tools and excellent books available to help you follow this advice. Simply Google *emotional intelligence* and watch what happens!

160. "You win with people." -Coach Woody Hayes

161. Always think twice before hitting Reply All.

162. Develop your wisdom when it comes to knowing when and when not to send people emails. Once decided, keep your emails short and to the point.

163. If you are in a leadership position, be very careful to avoid the habit of sending emails to your people late into the night! Know that they will feel obligated to check their emails into the evening which can create real stress and tension on the home front (and it can make you look unbalanced yourself)!

164. If you are up all night doing emails, save them as drafts and send them out after 6 a.m. You will look more balanced for sure, and avoid creating personal pressure that will affect your employees' performance.

165. There is no substitute for developing and practicing excellent listening skills . . .

. . . in everything you do at work.

. . . in everything you do with your significant other.

. . . in everything you do with your children.

. . . in everything you do in your life.

166. **Never nag people! It rarely, if ever, changes people's behavior, it is very annoying, and it makes you look bad!**

167. Remember people care how you much you care before they care how much you know . . . so look for ways to show people you care about them in real and meaningful ways.

168. When people know that we care about them and for them, they are more willing to follow us and work hard!

169. **Practice excellent telephone etiquette in all conversations and especially when leaving voicemail messages.**

170. Never eat or drink while doing business on the phone as it is both rude and messy. (And yes, they can tell.)

171. **Answer the phone with a smile . . . it will *always* show in your voice.**

172. **Make it a personal priority to know and remember people's names.**

173. Learn how to celebrate the success of other people in your organization!

174. Always be able to answer this question: "Why do people want to work with me?" And if you are having a hard time coming up with answers, you should consider seeking out feedback from others about how you need to improve!

175. If you are in a leadership position, adjust the question: **"Why are people willing to follow me?"**

176. It is a physiological fact that breakfast is the most important meal of the day. So make time for it!

177. Twenty-five percent: The typical average number of people who are satisfied with the quality and quantity of feedback they receive from their boss, based on our research!

178. Always look for opportunities to share credit with those who deserve it when things go right.

179. Learn to be honest with yourself!

180. Be the team player that knows how to bring people together, build a team, get things done, and create goodwill.

181. "Good leaders make people feel that they're at the very heart of things, not at the periphery. Everyone feels that he or she makes a difference to the success of the organization. When that happens people feel centered and that gives their work meaning." -Warren G. Bennis

182. Develop a real business strategy to use social media to enhance your business career and professional networks!

183. Fully understand the potential damaging impact that *unbridled* social media can have on your reputation, "brand," and career.

184. "When the trust account is high, communication is easy, instant, and effective." -Steven R. Covey

185. Develop excellent presentation skills and don't depend on PowerPoint or Prezi to make up for a lack of content, style, storytelling, or flare on your part!

186. When making a presentation that depends on technology or Internet access, always have a plan B!

187. When and if you experience technical difficulties during a presentation, apologize for the failure and move on.

188. Do not let people see you sweat, panic, or lose your cool when experiencing a technical difficulty during a presentation. Stay calm, poised, and use the opportunity to demonstrate your mastery of the subject matter and your awesome presentation and storytelling skills!

189. Learn to compliment others in public for a job well done and really mean it!

190. When dealing with vendors always know what you ultimately want from them and remember that almost everything is negotiable.

191. Remember that interpersonal conflicts are part of the workplace, so handle conflicts with the utmost care and professionalism . . . these conflicts will only escalate when left unchecked.

192. "The trouble with most of us is that we would rather be ruined by praise than saved by criticism." -Norman Vincent Peale

193. Take time to step in and be helpful when coworkers are "under siege" or simply buried with work. It sends a powerful message about who you are and the things that are truly important to you at work!

194. Never argue with or embarrass people in meetings or public settings!

195. Avoid spending an inordinate amount of time with glum, pessimistic, negative, and non-performing coworkers-these people a can be real "energy vampires" that pull you down.

196. Spending too much time with energy vampires can damage your motivation, attitude, job satisfaction, and reputation!

197. "If the blind lead the blind, both shall fall into the ditch," (Matthew 15:14b) so be really careful whom you follow!

198. Never hold a grudge against someone as it inhibits your ability to think clearly, make good decisions, and be at peace with yourself.

199. Be strong enough to forgive others when they have offended you, embarrassed you, disenfranchised you, or have taken advantage of you!

200. Never tell anyone at work something that you don't want anyone else to know.

201. Seek out the input of others in decisions that affect them. When people are part of the planning and decision-making process they become owners. When people own things they typically take care of them!

202. Never attack or put a coworker down in front of your boss. If a conflict exists between you and a coworker, stay focused on the facts of the situation and how the issue damages performance.

203. Don't be afraid to ask what might appear to be a dumb question as it is less damaging than cleaning up a dumb mistake!

204. "The best argument is that which seems merely an explanation." -Dale Carnegie

205. When leaving your phone number or email address in voicemail, always speak slowly, tell them you will repeat it twice, and then follow through—repeat it twice so you don't waste other people's time (who might otherwise have to listen to your message two or three times to get it right).

206. Remember there is a thin line between letting people know what you've accomplished and blowing your own horn to the point of being perceived as a braggart, show off, or egotist. Always walk this line *very* carefully.

207. "Become the kind of leader that people would follow voluntarily, even if you had no title or position." -Brian Tracy

208. Always be a real person of your word and always keep your commitments! Always!

209. Increase the amount of contact you have with your internal and external customers to better understand their needs and your actual performance.

210. "Coming together is a beginning. Keeping together is progress. Working together is success." -Henry Ford

211. Intentionally develop your conflict-resolution skills.

212. Remember how very powerful your words really are:
"Life and death are in the power of the tongue." (Proverbs 18:21)

213. "Remember that from the acorn of a problem grows the mighty oak tree of a problem when left to its own devices!" -Jack Simonetti

214. In one of our industry studies, nearly 70 percent of participants believed that workplace conflict is on the increase! Do you agree or disagree? Please write out your answer and explain why you believe this is the case. See what you can learn from your answer.

215. Primary reasons for an increase in workplace conflict include greater pressure to do more with less, dynamic workplace change, increased complexity, an increase in workplace drama, and ineffective leaders!

216. Know the difference between the two types of actual workplace conflicts—substantive conflicts and emotional conflicts.

Substantive conflicts occur when the issues driving disagreement are tangible, material, and reasonably concrete—things like goals, job assignments, timetables, processes, budgets, and other business-driven issues.

Emotional conflict on the other hand exists when there is tension between people because of personality differences or a breakdown in interpersonal relationships.

In both cases, conflict resolution is required, which is a **problem-solving process** designed to engage both parties in a fashion that illuminates the conflict. Master this skill for the good of your employer!

. . . and your family as well (and especially if you have teenagers).

217. Know that when a substantive conflict is ignored, it will quickly degenerate into a potentially ugly emotional conflict.

    Know also that emotional conflicts are much more difficult to resolve than our substantive conflicts.

218. If you are involved in a heated or emotional discussion, always count to 10 before responding. If you are involved in such a discussion and you are also *angry*, count to 30 before responding.

219. Most people agree that there is an upswing in workplace "drama" because of expansive and fragile egos, diverse workplace value systems, and unbridled competition. Remember: Excessive drama is a key indicator of a workplace that is not serious about getting results!

220. To solve any real organizational problem, or to remove any real performance barrier, you must get at the **real source** of the problem and not just the symptoms!

221. Know that getting people properly focused on the 12 Career Success and Survival Imperatives can have a powerful impact on reducing unwanted workplace drama.

222. "The two words *information* and *communication* are often used interchangeably, but they signify quite different things. *Information* is giving out; *communication* is getting through." -Journalist Sydney Harris

223. **A CRITICAL FACT:** The number-one source of workplace trouble and poor performance is communication break-downs!

Know that there are actually three kinds of workplace communications that are critical to the success of both individuals and organizations:

- ✓ Communications to give people the information they need to get their work done
- ✓ Communications to keep people informed about what's going on around them
- ✓ Upward communication so that people have a "voice"

224. **Huge Point:** Effective communications must take place to keep people around you properly informed so they can get <u>their</u> work done. Information concerning roles, goals, responsibilities, performance expectations, plans, rules, regulations, timetables, deadlines, and the like are critically important if people are to be successful at their jobs!

Do you have the information you need to successfully perform your job? If not, what information do you need and how do you plan to obtain it?

If you're in a leadership position, do the people who work with you and for you have the information they need to successfully perform their jobs? If not, what are you going to do to better equip them for success?

225. Huge Question: Are you and the people you work with "operating in the know"? Make sure that your organization takes every step to keep people informed of the things that are going on in your enterprise, especially in a rapidly changing environment!

FACT: In the absence of the ability to operate "in the know" with real information, people will gossip, fabricate, fill in, and allow their imaginations to run wild! These are all counterproductive behaviors that consume valuable time and energy.

226. Know that great organizations and leaders keep their people filled in on what is taking place in the organization as a whole as well as in their department and workgroup!

227. Do your very best to create a work environment where everyone has a voice. As you do this, know that having a voice means that people can freely share an idea, ask a question, express a concern, or identify a problem openly *and without fear*!

228. Whether or not members of your organization have a voice is a powerful indicator of how engaged, empowered, and energized they are to make a difference.

Know that if people don't have a voice, you are operating in a dysfunctional workplace that is not serious employee engagement or high performance!

229. Treat everyone with the utmost respect.

230. ... especially administrative assistants, secretaries, custodians, maintenance and security personnel, and all IT professionals.

231. Return phone calls promptly and develop a system to do so.

232. Here is an awesome and truly important quote: "The older I grow, the more I listen to people who don't say much." -Germaine Glidden

233. FACT: **"None of us is as smart as all of us!"** If we really believe this to be true, how should we approach planning, delegating, teambuilding, decision-making, and problem solving?

234. It is better to be a bit too loud than a bit too quiet when giving a presentation or running a meeting.

235. Take the time to get to know what makes each of your coworkers tick. This information is critically important to building awesome working relationships!

236. Remember co-workers' birthdays and anniversaries and make the effort to celebrate with song and food.

237. If someone is worth the effort of sending them a Christmas/greeting card, take the time to actually write a brief, warm, personal greeting instead of just signing it.

238. Don't wait for your superiors to recognize someone's efforts if they are truly noteworthy. Consider creating a "prize patrol" to unexpectedly celebrate people who go above and beyond the call of duty and do great work in your operation.

239. When someone takes the time to help you out, always ask: "What can I do to return the favor?" (And really mean it).

240. "Don't blow out another's candle, for it won't make yours shine brighter." -Jaachynma N.E. Agu

241. Remember that your attitude almost always affects your performance altitude, so stay positive!

242. Learn to look for opportunities in problems, letdowns, meltdowns, and big disappointments! They're usually there if you look hard enough and finding them can frequently offset some of the pain!

243. Never underestimate the power of a good story or the use of metaphors in trying to get people to actually remember something that is really important.

244. Always know the names of the people you are talking to when participating in a conference call, and call people by name. When asking a question or making a comment, always start by stating your name so that people on the call will know who is saying what!

245. Always double check when you hit the Mute button when participating in conference or GoToMeeting calls.

246. Know that it never hurts to have an outstanding working relationship with someone in your organization's HR department so you are in a position to seek counsel when HR issues arise (and they inevitably will).

247. Remember that ego problems are almost always at the root of getting professional and managerial personnel to work together as a team.

248. Say hello to people on elevators; it is a great place to put faces and names together in your organization.

249. "If you want to lift yourself up, lift up someone else." -Booker T. Washington

250. Get to know the needs, concerns, and personalities of your closest peers in your organization—those whom you need to get your work done.

251. "A winner is someone who recognizes their God-given talents, works his tail off to develop them into skills, and uses those skills to accomplish his goals." -Larry Bird

252. Remember that "arrogance" is an unacceptable character flaw that is a real turnoff to most people. Arrogance precludes great working relationships,

damages communications, prevents teamwork and cooperation, and can destroy effective decision-making and problem-solving!

253. When a friend gets promoted or starts a new job, take them to lunch to celebrate.

254. Don't use buzzwords like *virtual, strategic initiative, leverage, empowerment, paradigm, metric, disruptive* and/or *cross-functional* any more than necessary.

    ... Use words that will help you be understood in communicating with others.

255. Make people look good in front of their children and spouse at organizational functions when family members are in attendance.

256. Read a really good book on emotional intelligence... you'll learn a great deal about yourself and how to interact with those around you.

257. Don't get into a rut at work-from time to time, use your lunchtime as an opportunity to meet and get to know new and/or key people in your organization.

258. Keep a supply of $1 gift certificates around to use as on-the-spot mini-rewards for coworkers who do well (they'll appreciate the attention).

259. Read Dale Carnegie's book *How to Win Friends and Influence People*; the lessons are useful and timeless.

260. There is no substitute for having real enthusiasm and high energy for whatever you've been asked to do.

261. "The key to successful leadership today is influence, not authority." -Ken Blanchard

262. Learn how to explain complex things in very simple terms that everyone can understand.

263. If you are afraid of or uncomfortable about speaking in front of groups, seek out opportunities to do so to overcome your fear. Your long-term success depends on becoming better with this important organizational practice.

264. If you are comfortable and confident speaking in front of groups, don't be so comfortable that you fail to properly prepare or stop looking for ways to improve.

265. Never try to force "teamwork" in a situation where "cooperation" is all you really need to get strong performance.

266. Remember that failure comes with the territory of risk taking, leadership, innovation, and any change! When you meet a successful person, know that there's a very good chance they are very experienced with failure and maybe even experts on the subject despite what you might think!

It's a great exercise to ask a successful person that we look up to the following: "What is the biggest failure that you have had to overcome in your lifetime?" You will learn a lot by listening carefully to their response!

267. When failure happens, learn from it! Do not think of yourself as a failure because this type of thinking and negative self-talk damages your ability to bounce back!

268. Don't let fear of failure cause paralysis, inaction, or a "defeatist" attitude. "A positive attitude causes a chain reaction of positive thoughts, events, and outcomes. It is a catalyst and it sparks extraordinary results." -Wade Boggs

269. If you are gregarious, extroverted, outgoing, and like to talk, establish the habit of regularly having "quiet days" where you make listening your number-one priority! You will be more effective for doing so!

270. "Be quick to hear, slow to speak, and slow to anger." (James 1:19)

271. Always ask people to repeat back to you the instructions you've given them on important job assignments to ensure understanding (and always do the same when you're requested to act, as well).

272. Always pay close attention to nonverbal cues and body language, especially with people you do not know very well!

273. It has been said, "Never burn a bridge." Go one step further and make sure that you wisely invest time in "bridge maintenance"—it doesn't require any government funding dollars to do so!

274. Make it a priority to introduce yourself to people that you don't recognize at work. This simple act can go a long way in helping you build a strong people network within your organization.

275. Remember that respect and trust in any working relationship are difficult to re-establish once lost! Tread carefully!

276. Always introduce your coworkers and fellow organizational members to customers and explain how they, too, serve customer needs.

277. Develop a great working relationship with a talented information-technology professional.

278. Never confuse compliance with commitment. Compliance means that people do things because they have to. Commitment means that people will do things because they want to! This difference is significant to the success of any organizational effort!

279. "A leader is best when people barely know he exists. When his work is done, his aim fulfilled, they will say: We did it ourselves." -Lao Tzu

280. Don't keep looking at your watch or phone when you are having a conversation with someone. It's rude and it makes people feel insignificant or less than important.

281. If you do not have time to have a quality conversation with someone, be wise enough to stop and schedule a time when you can give him or her your complete and undivided attention.

282. Great relationships are almost always critical for repeat business, and great relationships take time, attention, and care: BE DILIGENT!

283. Get in the habit of bringing coffee, water, or soda for others when people gather from time to time to let people know that you care about them.

284. Keep a candy dish in your office and keep it full. People love it!

285. Learn how to effectively use flip charts to facilitate your group discussions and brainstorming or problem-solving meetings.

286. Never leave your marker pressed against the flipchart while you are thinking what to write—the maintenance people will not appreciate the permanent stain that you leave on the wall!

287. Make the development of great "people skills" an ongoing priority and life will get better for you both personally and professionally.

Learn how to effectively process and assess the actual behavior of the people you work with. To not do so limits your ability to build effective and meaningful working relationships with others.

Know yourself well enough to avoid this human tendency!

304. Do not rain on other people's parades!

305. Don't talk on the phone when someone is sitting in your office waiting to speak with you unless it is an emergency.

306. Remember what Winston Churchill said about the importance of your attitude: "A pessimist sees the difficulty in every opportunity; an optimist sees the opportunity in every difficulty."

307. When you find yourself in a situation where you don't know what to say, don't speak until you *do* know!

308. Trust is the foundation of any effective working relationship. You understand how trust can be broken, so make it a goal to never allow this to happen with the people you know, work with, and truly care about.

309. Know that fear in the workplace distracts people from doing their jobs, destroys teamwork, crushes innovation, and has a debilitating effect on communications!

Leaders and employees who create fear and anxiety in others must not be allowed to flourish and be promoted in an organization that is serious about excellence!

310. Whether it is professional or personal, "Don't let the sun go down on your anger." (Ephesians 4:26)

311. Always keep your ego in check in every situation.

312. Always take great care in developing work schedules as they affect people's personal lives in very real and serious ways.

313. Be friendly to everyone. There is nothing stopping you from doing so!

314. Always keep in touch with a couple of corporate recruiters/headhunters throughout your career. You never know when you just might need them!

315. In a snowstorm, clean off a coworker's car in the parking lot for them.

316. Control your temper at work because when you lose it, you could lose more than your temper.

317. Know that there is a thin line between being "intense" and being unhinged and unbalanced in the eyes of others.

318. Never complain about management, your pay, or company policy in front of people at work . . . It won't change a thing and it just might come back to haunt you!

319. It is been said, "Treat people the way you want to be treated." But it is more important to learn to treat people the way that they want to be treated.

ONGOING LEARNING AND PERFORMANCE IMPROVEMENT

"The measure of success is not whether you have a tough problem to deal with, but whether it is the same problem you had last year."
-John Foster Dulles

320. Know that human performance is always a function of three critically important things: Talent. Motivation. Support.

Talent means that a person has the requisite skills, knowledge, and abilities to be successful at a particular task or endeavor.

Motivation means that a person has the requisite work ethic, drive, energy, and passion to be successful at a particular task or endeavor.

Support means that a person has the requisite information, sanction, access, processes, resources, and decision-making authority to be successful at a particular task or endeavor.

321. When you want to improve your performance or the performance of one of your people, use the intersection of these three features as a diagnostic and planning tool to determine where performance improvement is going to come from!

322. Remember: "Insanity: doing the same thing over and over again and expecting different results." -Albert Einstein

323. "Anyone who stops learning is old, whether at 20 or 80. Anyone who keeps learning stays young. The greatest thing in life is to keep your mind young."
    -Henry Ford

324. **The three most important questions for real success at WORK -** To increase my effectiveness and performance as a leader/professional, what do I need to . . .
KEEP DOING?
START DOING?
STOP DOING?

325. **The three most important questions for success in MARRIAGE -** To increase my effectiveness and performance as a spouse, what do I need to . . .
KEEP DOING?
START DOING?
STOP DOING?

326. **The three most important questions for success in PARENTING -** To increase my effectiveness and performance as a parent, what do I need to . . .
KEEP DOING?
START DOING?
STOP DOING?

327. Keep your technical skills in your discipline up to speed at all times! To not do so is to open the door for trouble and technical obsolescence!

328. To better understand the power and potential pitfalls of team decision-making and consensus building, watch Sidney Lumet's 1957 classic *12 Angry Men.* It will be well worth 96 minutes of your time and there's a good chance you'll learn something important about yourself!

329. Update your resume at least once a year regardless of how secure you *think* your job happens to be. Updating your resume is a good way to look at where you've been with your career, and a good reminder of where you just might want to go!

330. Be willing to take on new assignments that your organization considers important so you can take on a new challenge, stretch your skills, expand your experience, and make new contacts. These outcomes are career enhancing!

331. *"Find out what it is in life that you don't do well, and then don't do that thing!"* -The World's Most Interesting Man (Advice: Play to your strengths)

332. Keep your office/workspace clean and organized, as it is a direct reflection of you and will help increase your personal effectiveness and productivity. Don't allow yourself the excuse that you know exactly where everything is because, while it may be true, there is still a cost in image, as a disorganized workspace is associated with a lack of care, wasted time, and more.

333. Always look for ways to make it easier to get things done for both yourself and others. You deserve it and others will greatly appreciate the fact that you are helping them get their work done!

334. Develop a real relationship with an accountability partner that you trust and meet with them regularly for counsel, encouragement, and accountability. Most successful changes in any arena of life require accountability! Who's holding you accountable to be the best YOU that you can be?

335. Remember these important words when taking on a new project or improvement initiative: "There is no substitute for preparation when entering the arena!" -Football Coach Tom Amstutz

336. Take regular time for personal reflection so that you know yourself. It is critically important to know your professional and personal strengths and weaknesses as well as likes and dislikes . . . To not know yourself is to open the door to taking on activities and engaging in work that doesn't play to your strengths.

337. Always know what is really going on around you and how you and your operation are performing. Organizational "surprises" can be very, very painful.

338. Set up a system to regularly monitor your personal performance so you always know where you stand against what you are being paid to accomplish. This self-monitoring and self-assessing behavior is what frequently separates good performers from great performers!

339. Remember: "Life is all about improvement, whether it's as a singer, a musician, or a songwriter, or, you know, any of the other hats that we wear . . . hopefully we're just getting better." -Glenn Frey of the Eagles

340. Stay calm at all times, as losing control of your emotions at work can create real and unanticipated problems. It is very hard to find examples of anyone losing control of their emotions at work and enhancing their career trajectory! Think about it.

341. Interview a successful person in your profession annually to explore the challenges they face, current industry trends, and their secrets to success. Oh, and buy them lunch for their time and investment in you!

342. Know and understand the barriers that prevent people from developing their talents in your workplace. Make yourself aware of your own barriers while you're at it!

343. What is the most important skill for your success? Write it down and explain why it is so utterly important.

344. Now create a personal-development plan: identify two or three specific skills that are key to improving your performance and create a specific action plan

that you can follow. Implement this plan and create accountability for sticking to it. Otherwise, it is simply a wish list for things you are hoping to change.

345. **Wanting, wishing, and hoping for talent development, without a specific action plan, is not an effective improvement strategy!**

346. According to our research, here are the things that will prevent you from implementing your plan:

  ✓ Time pressures
  ✓ Lack of feedback and coaching
  ✓ Lack of self-reflection and self-assessment
  ✓ Ego issues and over-confidence
  ✓ A lack of commitment and ongoing motivation
  ✓ Lack of accountability for change
  ✓ Having a bad boss

  For you to develop world-class talent you need to be able to overcome these barriers/obstacles to your development!

347. Great leaders are typically great readers! Since reading is a critical part of most of our lives, look for ways to accelerate your reading speed and you will quickly become more productive.

348. Once your performance has plateaued at a high level in a given position, don't be afraid to ask your boss for additional responsibilities, cross training/cross-functional learning, or special learning assignment

opportunities! The more diverse your talent base, the greater your career trajectory!

349. Remember that adult learners learn by doing! Doing always accelerates real learning!

350. Gautama Buddha once said, *"I never see what has been done; I only see what remains to be done."*

We all tend not to stop and appreciate the things that we have accomplished. If we are not careful we miss out on the joy of feeling good about our achievements and learning from these experiences!

So, regularly take time to recognize your achievements, and it doesn't hurt to verbally acknowledge those of your coworkers, as well!

351. Listen to recorded books during your commute using any number of easy-to-use technology platforms.

Listen to good fiction books to help you relax, expand your mind, and for pure enjoyment. Listen to nonfiction books on things of importance to your life to be better informed, well-read, and to help you with your personal and professional development. Your public library is a great free resource and as a general rule very user-friendly!

352. Identify and break bad work habits that get in the way of better performance. So, do you have a bad work habit right now that you need to fix? Be aware of that bad work habit and take real steps to fix it, otherwise you are

courting less than optimal performance and career advancement trouble!

353. "Be the change that you wish to see in the world." -Mahatma Gandhi

354. "Like iron sharpens iron, so one person can sharpen another." (Proverbs 27:17) So remember, you are in the blacksmith business whether you realize it or not!

355. Always have someone in your life that you are mentoring, not only to share your wisdom and experience but also to remind you where you have been.

356. Remember that a mistake is only a mistake the first three times—after that it is a personal habit and a lifestyle choice that has become part of who you are. Learn from your mistakes by understanding the causes and factors that will prevent you from repeating them. Take time to analyze and think through your performance failings when they occur so you can actually learn from them.

357. It has been said, ***"Everything is negotiable!"*** If this axiom is true, each one of us has a responsibility to ourselves and to our employers to become master negotiators!

358. Set the goal of improving your negotiation skills and know that there is a plethora of great online resources, books, and formal training programs out there for doing so. You might even be able to negotiate with your boss to have them pay!

359. Be reminded that if you cannot successfully lead your own life in a meaningful and effective way, it will be exceedingly difficult to lead others!

360. Attend at least one leadership or "people skills" training/development program each year to sharpen your talents and remind yourself of the importance of these critical, career-enhancing skills.

361. Seek out community service opportunities and activities that you can use to sharpen your skills, improve your attitude, and make a difference where you live!

Engage in *select* community service activities that create goodwill for your employer, help meet community needs, and match up well with your personal values, skills, and interests. If you don't do it, who will?

362. Encourage your employer to create a formal employee volunteer service program. Our research shows that when employers have formal employee volunteer programs, employees feel proud of their employers, and the programs provide an opportunity to give back to their community and build an organization's image and business networks!

363. Know that community service can be a great developmental experience for those who volunteer. Community service reminds us how fortunate we are to have a job, our health, food, and shelter. Community service reminds us how fortunate we are to have people in our lives who care about us!

Community service can also help us stay humble, realize our blessings, and keep our feet firmly planted on the ground.

364. And community service can help us develop and refine our talents as servant-leaders. So never underestimate the power and potential impact community service can have on you, your employer, and your community!

365. Community service can teach your children the importance of serving others at an early age so look for opportunities where children or grandchildren can join in! As your children and grandchildren grow, seek out service opportunities that will match up with their current development needs and desires!

366. On the other hand, never allow too much community service to consume time that is really needed for your family.

367. Set up cross-training activities for yourself with departments that you need to get your work done. This cooperative work can help you truly understand what they are up against and what they need from you. Building relationships with these folks will, in the long run, help you get your work done and become more effective and empathetic in working with others!

368. "Personally I'm always ready to learn, although I do not always like being taught." -Winston Churchill

369. Learn some invaluable lessons on the importance of coaching and accountability by watching the 2011 Oscar award–winning film, *The King's Speech*. This

epic film chronicles the struggles of England's King George VII as he attempts to overcome a lifelong impediment that is damaging his ability to lead his nation in a time of extreme peril. Key lesson: We all need help to improve—even kings!

370. Pay close attention to and learn from the mistakes of others to see what might be learned. Never throw away these important opportunities to learn.

371. Make it a point to teach your "tricks of the trade" and "best practices" to the people you work with who really want to learn and develop themselves.

372. Make sure that you know about and make use of all of the training and development resources that your organization has available.

373. While no one wants to fail, failure can have some positive consequences: "Failure is good. It's fertilizer! Everything I've learned about coaching, I've learned from making mistakes." -Coach Rick Pitino

374. Workplace coaching is all about helping other people achieve SUCCESS that they couldn't achieve without the training, feedback, encouragement, reflection, and accountability provided by their coach. Take full advantage of this awesome truth both as a workplace coach and a workplace player!

375. Review progress against your SMART goals weekly, monthly, quarterly, and annually and make ongoing adjustments in your efforts that reflect the changing circumstances of your environment.

376. Spearhead a team effort to improve a key operating process that is critical to your operation's performance and overall success.

377. Consider pursuing additional formal education that will strengthen your ability to get better results and be a more complete and competitive professional.

378. Take the opportunity to conduct a training program for your organization on a topic in which you either have expertise or wish to develop expertise. There is no substitute for becoming a content expert on an important skill that is necessary for your organization's success!

379. Do not develop an over-reliance on your boss or your organization's HR department for your professional development because it is ultimately *your* responsibility. The onus for your development is squarely on your shoulders—and that is exactly where it should be!

380. When attending formal training classes, sit up front, be an active, involved learner, ask great questions,

develop an action plan for implementing key ideas, and take what you've learned and teach it to others.

381. After attending a formal training program, set implementation goals, create accountability for change, and make the new behaviors part of your formal performance review with your boss. Without this action and accountability, there's a very good chance that you will not implement what you've learned and get little or no return-on-investment for yourself or your enterprise!

382. **Idea:** Write short monthly performance reports for your boss detailing your activities, achievements, changing circumstances, and results. These reports can improve communications, keep your boss informed, help you stay aligned, and make it easier for your boss to deliver better performance reviews.

383. "Never doubt that a small group of thoughtful, committed people can change the world. Indeed. It is the only thing that ever has." - Margaret Mead

384. Never underestimate the power of a well-written thank-you note to let people know how much you appreciate them!

385. Proactively take the initiative to work with your boss to develop an effective and accurate method to formally review your performance at least twice a year for input, feedback, alignment, and adjustment.

386. Ignorance is not a legitimate excuse for poor performance in most organizations. If there are things you need to know to do your job, and do it well, seek out the information you need NOW! Not knowing what to do and how to do it in any position can create real trouble for you and your organization!

387. At least once a year take the opportunity to visit a vendor, customer, or trade association that is known for excellence to see and explore for yourself what they are doing and how they are doing it on a firsthand basis.

388. After a customer or systems failure, crisis, meltdown, or blowup, always conduct an "after-action debrief" to understand the root cause of the occurrence. It is vital to identify specifically what needs to be done to prevent a reoccurrence. Fight the temptation to just walk away, ignore it, or sweep the failure under the rug. LEARN FROM THE EXPERIENCE!

389. "Progress is impossible without change, and those who cannot change their minds cannot change anything." -George Bernard Shaw

390. According to our research, rapid organizational change can quickly expose a person's:

   ✓ Ineffective communication and listening skills
   ✓ Poor time management

✓ Inability to clarify direction and performance expectations
✓ Ineffective interpersonal and team skills
✓ Inability to handle stress!

391. Once a year formally seek out performance feedback from the 5–10 people you depend on the most to get your work done. Ask them what's working, what's not working, and what you need to start doing to become more effective!

392. When it comes to change, remember this important quote: ***"Not to decide is to decide."*** -Harvey Cox

393. *"No problem can withstand the assault of sustained thinking."* -Voltaire

394. Volunteer with an elementary school reading program to help your community, polish your coaching skills, and to stay in touch with the things that are really important.

395. Establish a set time each week to work on an emerging skill or one that you want to polish. Stick to the schedule, focus intensely on your personal learning like you are cramming for an exam, and practice, practice, practice!

396. Develop expertise in the skill of "process mapping" and use this talent regularly to improve a key work process that impacts your ability to deliver desired outcomes.

397. To use or allow others to use inefficient or "broken processes" is to waste time, breed frustration, and damage your credibility if you're in a leadership

position! Set a goal of improving at least one key operating process per quarter in your operation.

398. Make it a priority to turn any customer problem into a double-edged opportunity—impress the customer with your commitment to them and use the situation to illuminate an organizational shortcoming that can be addressed and fixed. Difficulties that our customers have with us are actually opportunities for us to improve our performance and build customer loyalty if we are serious about making real change happen fast on the customer's behalf!

399. When coming to a group decision of any consequence, always assign one or two people to serve as the Designated Devil's Advocate (DDA) to challenge the group's thinking along the decision path and to ask tough/taboo questions.

400. When groups make decisions, test their commitment to a particular course of action and press the group to justify their plan or decision until the question *"Is this really what we all agree is optimal?"* is answered.

401. When things are going particularly bad on a given day, call a five-minute "time-out" to get co-workers together and regroup. Anyone in the group should be able to call a regroup time-out after a set of clear guidelines have been agreed to by everyone.

402. Morale, job satisfaction, and turnover issues are almost always driven by the very same set of factors that affect and drive performance. If you are ever given the assignment to improve job satisfaction or workforce morale, focus your efforts in the right place!

You are best served by focusing on *how to create a high-performance workplace* and *providing people with the tools they need* to deliver results. If you do this effectively, job satisfaction and employee morale will almost always improve!

403. Share great articles, newspapers clippings, and video/audio clips with the people you work with to stimulate their thoughts about issues that are important for people in your line of work.

404. When discussing how to improve individual performance always focus on the individual's behavior and not their attitude. Discussions of attitude become very subjective very quickly so instead discuss *behaviors* that are observable, real, and tangible.

405. From time to time record yourself making a presentation. When you review it you just might be surprised at what you learn.

406. Create a "balanced scorecard" for yourself so you both clearly identify the metrics that are important to your success and understand the variables that affect or drive your performance. Developing these metrics will help you focus your energy, time, and resources on the things that are truly important for your long-term success!

Keep your scorecard simple, keep it updated, and after you learn how to use it wisely, ask your boss to make it a part of your formal performance review.

407. Keep sharpening your computer skills using the most efficient means possible, from training programs to asking your children to tutor you one-on-one on a

new computer application that might help you become more efficient at work or maybe even a better parent. (It's a humbling but effective exercise.)

408. Do not go to training classes unless they will actually help you develop a skill you need to improve your performance or help you polish an existing skill. Organizations and individuals frequently waste lots of valuable time and money with good training intentions but little real return-on-investment.

409. Remember that organizational change initiatives are frequently ineffective because they fail to clearly define a desired outcome and/or what individuals and work groups need to do differently for success. Always develop clear direction and clear behavioral guidelines for any desired change.

410. Don't expect significant downsizing and large-scale restructuring initiatives to provide real long-term improvement in your operation's long-term growth and profitability.

411. KEY POINT: Always know why people in your organization get fired!

412. One of the biggest lessons learned from our research on high-performance leaders is this simple fact:

You are personally responsible for your personal and professional development!

413. To reach your full potential as a professional requires a **real plan** and **real action** and should include some of the following 10 practices that emerge from our research . . .

414. Conduct a personal SWOT Analysis of your strengths and weaknesses and how you stack up in the current opportunities and threats that exist in your organization and in your current position.

415. Learn to seek out honest and accurate performance feedback from a wide variety of trusted sources.

416. Read relevant materials for exposure to new practices, trends, and relevant industry information.

417. Take sufficient time on a regular basis for self-reflection and self-appraisal—look in the mirror and identify areas needing work and take action.

418. Recruit, hire, promote, and surround yourself with talented people who can help develop your thinking and push your performance up a notch.

419. Set a goal to attend at least one formal continuing-education program, workshop, and seminar annually to refresh existing skills and to acquire new skills.

420. Secure a membership in a top-flight professional or trade association that can provide you with new job-development opportunities and industry networks and connections.

421. Mentor and coach members of your own organization and connect with organizational members outside of your department to learn more about what is going on across the enterprise.

422. Benchmark and observe the practices of effective leaders both inside and outside of your organization to stimulate your creativity, learning, and to generate ideas on how you can improve.

423. Find an accountability partner and a mentor (or mentors) who can provide the feedback, counsel, and accountability that is necessary for real change in one's life.

424. If you want to round out and/or refresh your overall business and leadership skill set but do not have time to go back to school for more coursework or to complete an MBA, get your hands on The Great Courses—Critical Business Skills for Success. This five-part sixty-lecture course will provide you with a tremendous overview of business strategy, operations, marketing, accounting and finance, and leadership and organizational behavior that will have a considerable impact on your ability to deliver better results! Go to http://www.thegreatcourses.com

425. It is imperative that selection, promotion, demotion, compensation, development assignments, and termination decisions be tied to people's actual performance for your organization to be successful!

426. Be wary of telling people to improve their performance by just working harder. If they don't have the requisite talent they very well may take your advice, but in doing so, produce even more bad performance—and faster than before!

427. If you find yourself lacking the skill you need to do your job, don't wait for your boss or organization for help ... take action yourself to fill the need.

428. Subscribe to the best publication in your field that will help keep you up to date and schedule time to read it regularly.

429. Sit on a volunteer board of directors for an organization you truly care about so you can expand and hone your strategic thinking and acumen.

430. Look for ways to help your customers grow their businesses, connect with new customers, save money, and improve their processes. You will be investing in your own success!

431. Learn and perfect how to "sell" goods, services, ideas, decisions, change, plans, and yourself.

432. Have the discipline and strength to be brave enough to "kill" an improvement initiative when it is clear to all that it is not going to work.

433. Take proactive steps to ensure that people in all staff positions perform truly value-added work that supports the mission of the organization. Remember that these positions when not properly managed will increase organizational overhead while at the same time creating bureaucracy that can make it difficult for contributors to get real work done!

434. In writing a written performance appraisal, always remember that what is written is what is remembered!

435. Never jump to conclusions in interpersonal or workplace conflicts . . . the landing can be very painful.

436. Remember that the tenets and practices of Total Quality Management are timeless, so the fact that TQM has fallen from the limelight doesn't mean it can't serve you and your organization well.

437. "Experience teaches only the teachable." -Aldous Huxley

438. Occasionally conduct meetings where all the participants are asked to stand for the entire meeting. Standing causes people to pay attention and keep the meeting on track. However, don't take the chairs out of the meeting room because that wastes time.

439. Know yourself well enough to avoid activities that put you in a bad mood, especially before important one-on-one meetings, presentations, problem-solving activities, major decisions, and performance reviews (unless it is something that you need to overcome).

440. Remember that angry emails, tantrums, change-or-die speeches, memos, and verbal mandates rarely, if ever change people's actual behavior. They might make you feel better but know that little if anything will actually change and your situation might even get worse!

441. Learn how to read and understand your organization's balance sheet and profit/loss statement.

442. When faced with making major decisions, seek the counsel of wise people you trust who can offer real, experienced and objective insight.

443. Keep a notepad next to your bed; great ideas frequently come in the night.

444. When you think changes need to be made, always do your homework!

445. Always take great care of and do preventive maintenance on the tools you need to get your work done.

446. Learn to reward yourself when you do a good job.

447. Slow down. You will live longer according to what we know about stress and physiology!!

448. Become actively involved in a professional association that can help you hone your skills and expand your business contacts but never at the expense of getting your job done.

449. Always have a confidant in your organization one level above and two levels below your current position so you can really know what is going on in your enterprise.

450. Volunteer annually to participate in a high school or college "shadow program" to let a student follow you around for a day (you both will learn a lot).

451. Take your children to work with you once a year so they can see your daily world and so that your co-workers can see you in your role as a parent.

452. Keep a very accurate file of your achievements and failures.

453. Forge a "feedback agreement" with your boss on what parts of your performance need feedback, what kinds of feedback, and how often so they will know how to best help you stay on track and improve your performance.

454. Don't wait to be "empowered" before making a decision if you are trying to fix a critical customer problem. Actions always speak louder than words to customers and losing a customer to a situation that could have been fixed is just plain dumb.

455. When attempting to solve a problem, make sure that you have identified the right problem to solve before you move forward. In problem-solving, haste really does make waste.

456. Go to any major sporting event and you will see signs that read, *No Spectators Allowed!* Similarly, in the modern workplace, we need to make sure that everyone is a participant, engaged, and a co-owner of the team's activity whether it is solving a problem,

improving a process, or making a change! Put the same sign up in your workplace and live by it.

457. Be extremely careful about implementing "half-baked" ideas, plans, policies, procedures, and/or programs that do not make sense to you with the people that will have to live with them.

458. Make it a meaningful practice to know the **WHY** behind the **WHAT**!

459. When using committees and task forces at work, design the membership and the size of the team to meet the specific demands of the actual project! When using committees and task forces at work, keep the number of members small unless there are compelling reasons to do otherwise! Smaller groups can move faster, meet more easily, and have greater levels of accountability for desired outcome!

460. Remember that workplace "quick fixes" are almost always neither!

461. "Tell me and I forget, teach me and I may remember, involve me and I learn." -Benjamin Franklin

462. Less than 20 percent of all change initiatives achieve their desired outcomes, which means that expectations are either set too high or these change initiatives are poorly planned and executed!

463. Take time to think and plan long-term about your career on a quarterly basis as careers go fast!

464. Set the realistic goal of learning one new vocabulary word each week and use it. (There is a correlation between having a strong vocabulary and career success.)

465. Always be a mentor to someone who needs your support, guidance, wisdom, and encouragement.

466. When you go to work, don't leave your imagination at home.

467. "Change is the ultimate team sport!" -Dr. Tim Stansfield

468. "People who work together will win, whether it be against complex football defenses, or the problems of modern society." -Vince Lombardi

469. Here's the challenge: driving any change/problem-solving initiative is always in addition to your day job! This fact means that anyone's performance can be damaged when we are asked to take on too many change initiatives at one point in time!

470. Ask yourself this question: When is a change truly needed? Answer: When things are not working. Why aren't things working? Because you have a problem! **Critically Important Point**: The change process is simply problem-solving, so we are better served when we approach change as a problem-solving exercise and we engage those who have the greatest insight and know how to solve the problem! Reframing any

change as a team-based, problem-solving adventure is one of the smartest things a leader can do.

471. People can easily resist and/or fear change. However, people more easily understand that problems have to be solved, especially when their livelihood depends on it. Learn to frame change as problems to solve!

472. When entering any change/problem-solving initiative, start with the model that is universally known and understood by everyone involved in the change! If your organization has a formal improvement process such as Lean, Six-Sigma, Kaizen, Ford QOS, or the like, you need to know and thoroughly understand it!

473. In our analysis of over a thousand change initiatives across every industry in America, the key predictor of success was WHO was leading the project. To be successful in the long haul, you must be a skilled and effective change agent—one who facilitates and drives problem-solving and improvement! It is a talent you must master given this important research finding!

474. "Leadership is the capacity and will to rally men and women to a common purpose and the character which inspires confidence." -Field Marshal Bernard Montgomery

475. Complicated and overly sophisticated change initiatives that cannot be executed in reality are doomed from the get-go! Plan and operate in reality!

476. Any change worth making is worth making faster!

477. Remember: Any time you attempt a change effort that does not deliver results, your credibility and career opportunities are not moving in the right direction! Do not play around with change initiatives—**any change is worth doing right or it is pointless**!

478. To use a football metaphor, think about change as a two-minute drill. You are behind on the scoreboard, time is of the essence, and you must score if you are to win! Never enter a change initiative without clearly defining what success looks like and what score you need to win!

479. Once you define "winning," it is imperative to put together a "scouting report" on what you and the members of your team are up against in attempting to make this change! Make sure that you know and understand your opponents!

480. Set up a scoreboard to keep track of the goal, players, activities, timelines, performance, and progress toward the achievement of your desired outcome!

481. Know that without a sense of urgency, the likelihood of success in any change effort is very, very low.

482. You need to design the change that will solve your problem with the input and ownership of the members of your team! Own it-Live it!

483. For any change effort to be successful you must have the right players involved in the process at each and every step! Make sure that your people have the requisite talent, motivation, and support to be effective in this change effort!

484. "It's not the will to win but the will to prepare that makes the difference in a big game." -Coach Paul "Bear" Bryant

485. Think of each activity in your change model as a play that has to be executed in a timely fashion with each person knowing and performing their role!

486. Performance of each activity or "play" in your change model must be measured and critiqued to ensure progress! Execution of each play leads to progress!

487. Always monitor and measure performance on an ongoing basis so you are in a position to coach and reinforce progress and desired behaviors!

488. Remember you are the quarterback: If you are in charge of the change, you need to energize your people, communicate above the roar of the crowd, create ownership, and make adjustments quickly!

489. While you might be making changes to a business strategy, process, IT platform, or operating procedure, in the end, individuals must change their individual behavior or you are wasting everyone's time! Bottom line: If individuals do not change their individual behavior you will not have a real change!

490. At the end of any change initiative, conduct a "post-game" analysis to determine what you and the members of your team learned during the change process and to develop lessons that can be shared with others in your organization! This "organizational learning" can be an invaluable tool for accelerating future change initiatives.

491. Make sure that changes stick: Reinforce appropriate behavior both as a team and for individuals and remember what Harvard Business Professor John Kotter said, "One of the four top reasons for (change) failure is claiming victory before the war is over."

492. Learn how to celebrate success!

493. When you are given a compliment for a job well done, never throw it back in someone's face by saying, "It's no big deal," or "It's just my job." Learn how to accept and appreciate compliments and positive feedback from others by simply looking them in the eye, smiling, and saying "thank you!"

494. Learn how to accept constructive criticism by truly listening and being open minded. Defensiveness, argumentativeness, and close-mindedness are all attributes of emotionally unintelligent people.

495. When you receive negative feedback and constructive criticism write it down, take a step back, and review this information when you are not in the heat of battle. BE COACHABLE!

496. Criticism and negative feedback are never easy to hear, let alone accept! Yet we have to learn to process this important information as this is how we learn and make adjustments to improve! -Expanded from a thought from Norman Vincent Peale

497. Learn how to embrace your organization's formal performance appraisal process because our extensive research shows that employees who do so are more likely to engage in activities that lead to higher levels of performance.

498. A primary factor that will influence the quality of your formal performance appraisals is the quality of your ongoing working relationship with your boss! The better your working relationship with your boss the more meaningful the formal performance appraisal process becomes!

499. So make it easy for your boss to identify and document your value-added role, goals, and responsibilities for the upcoming performance period by staying aligned on an ongoing basis!

500. Remember that, "Feedback is the breakfast of champions!" -Ken Blanchard

501. Establish a "feedback/coaching contract" with your boss that details how often you would like to meet to discuss your performance, update your boss on what is going on, and to realign your priorities during the performance period.

502. Once your feedback contract is established, stick with it for at least one year and see what you learn about yourself and your boss!

503. When it is time for your written performance appraisal, always submit a self-appraisal to your boss at least a week ahead of time that highlights your key contributions, areas needing improvement, and personal development plans for the upcoming performance period.

504. When it is time for your face-to-face performance review with your boss, come with a mindset to listen, learn, and absorb to determine the extent to which you and your boss are on the same page! And come to the session with your written assessment of what you are going to do to improve your performance and get better results during the next performance period.

505. One week after your formal, face-to-face performance review with your boss, schedule a time for a follow-

up session to review the content of the assessment, to solidify your realigned role, goals, and responsibilities for the upcoming performance period, and your game plan for success!

TRUE GRIT PROFESSIONALISM AND CHARACTER

"Knowing is not enough; we must apply. Willing is not enough; we must do." - Goethe

506. Never allow yourself to "whine" under any circumstances. Nothing good can come from whining and especially at work, home, or in public!

507. "If the people you are hanging out with don't share your vision, dreams, and big ideas, then you're hanging out with the wrong people." -Football Coach Jason Candle

508. Make it a real priority and mission to apply your results-oriented professional talents to your role as a spouse, parent, friend, neighbor, and community servant so you maximize your performance in these other truly important roles in your life.

509. Don't be known as a gossip, rumormonger, naysayer, wet blanket, worrywart, cynic, pessimist, or a weaver

of woe. These are the characteristics of people that others do not choose or wish to work with, or even be around for that matter!

510. If you are considering getting a tattoo on your face, neck, head, or on the back of your hands, take the time to think long-term to determine if there are potential career consequences for doing so. *Think Before You Ink!*

511. Also, always think through the long-term career ramifications of body piercings.

512. To better understand the importance of making good decisions on a daily basis, read Malcolm Gladwell's best-selling book, *The Tipping Point.* It has powerful lessons about the cumulative effect good and bad decisions can have on lives and careers. Note: All of his books are quite remarkable and will cause you to look at things quite differently at many levels.

513. *Always do the right thing!* And if you are not sure what the right thing is, ask your spouse, dad, mom, pastor, rabbi, priest, mullah, high school teacher, or children! Seeking this counsel can offer great insight, clarity, and accountability.

514. Never forget that your actions speak louder than your words. So which actions of yours speak positively about you? Which actions speak poorly about you?

515. "I know of no single formula for success. But over the years I have observed that some attributes of leadership are universal and are often about finding

ways of encouraging people to combine their efforts, their talents, their insights, their enthusiasm, and their inspiration to work together." -Queen Elizabeth II

516. Work to live, so you don't live to work.

Striking a good balance between work and life is one of the greatest gifts you can give to yourself and to those around you! Don't become a slave to your job to the point of losing touch with the truly important things in life! This can easily happen to anyone so be *careful* and *diligent!*

517. Make a conscientious effort to live beneath your means.

This lifestyle choice will have a powerful impact on your levels of stress, fear of workplace failure, and how well you sleep at night!

Here is a personal suggestion: Use a financial planner that tends to be conservative, shares your value system, and that you have regular contact with outside of your financial planning relationship! It is important to know them as a person, what makes them tick, and their priorities as they can and will have a powerful impact on your financial destiny!

518. Remember that there is a direct link between your health and your ability to *lead a long, active, productive, and fulfilling life.*

519. Know that the best way to avoid the pains and hardships of losing weight is to proactively develop a plan to not gain weight in the first place. Yes, you can do this, and the younger you start, the better!

520. Remember that there is a direct link between your health and your ability to *achieve higher levels of performance in the workplace!*

521. In one of our studies on high performance and health, a large sample of participants cited a number of powerful benefits that were associated with being healthy and consistently making healthy lifestyle choices:

   ✓ Increased energy and drive
   ✓ Greater physical stamina and endurance
   ✓ Lower levels of stress
   ✓ Increased cognitive and thinking capabilities
   ✓ An overall increase in productivity
   ✓ A more positive attitude

522. If you are struggling with your weight, most experts agree that a two-pronged approach of both diet and exercise are necessary for effective weight reduction. Do some homework, get the facts, consult your doctor, and consider your options.

   Now use this critical information to put together an Action Plan that can be implemented just like you would if this were a business situation needing change! Remember that you have the talent and tools to do it and that you can do anything that you set your mind, heart, and soul to doing!

523. Losing weight is a team sport!

Build a team around you with people who can encourage, motivate, and hold you accountable.

524. Read the 2001 Harvard Business Review Classic *The Making of a Corporate Athlete* for some tremendous insight on the importance of the link between your health and your ability to compete in the modern workplace! This article will chronicle the link between your mind, emotions, body, and spirit and your ability to achieve superior and sustained performance in the workplace.

525. Research shows that when people get too busy, there is a tendency to stop exercising, eat poorly, and not get enough sleep. Answer this question for yourself:

How does being too busy and moving too fast affect my health and my lifestyle choices?

526. Do not underestimate the importance of allowing your heart, mind, spirit, and body to "recover" after you have gone through a period of intense and demanding work. Don't kid yourself, we all need an opportunity to take a time-out, catch our breath, and recharge our batteries after working big hours week in and week out or launching/completing a major project!

527. Never forget that "Recovering energy is as important as expanding it!" -Jim Loehr and Tony Schwartz

528. To get good exercise as a busy working professional, you need to create a PLAN to create a real PROGRAM for yourself!

529. Establish and implement an exercise program that works for you, your schedule, and your body clock. Make this program a habit as the benefits are incalculable in every area of your life!

530. "*Impossible* is just a word thrown around by small men who find it easier to live in the world they have been given than to explore the power they have to change it. Impossible is not a fact. It's an opinion. Impossible is not a declaration. It's a dare. Impossible is potential. Impossible is temporary. Impossible is nothing!" -Mohammad Ali

531. Get a training partner and work out regularly together to help you develop the habit. A training partner's accountability, insight, and encouragement can be priceless! And remember that when you consistently share this experience with another person, you'll learn a great deal about each other that will put you in a position to be peer mentors and accountability partners in other areas of your life.

532. Consider buying or going on Craigslist and purchasing workout equipment that will allow you to work out at home when you watch TV or do your reading. Lightly used exercise equipment is for sale everywhere and can be a great investment! Convenience is key!

533. While we all have different physiological needs for sleep, most experts agree that most people need a minimum of seven hours of sleep at least five nights a week so you'll have the energy you need to compete and perform.

While we all have different body clocks, more and more research points to the fact that it is better to go to bed early and wake up early. Bonus: rising early also makes it easier to get your workday off to a quicker and more focused start!

534. Take short breaks every two hours during your workday to get up, stretch, and move around to give both your body and brain an opportunity to refresh, reframe, and refocus!

535. Drink lots of water every day!

536. If you are healthy enough, be an American Red Cross blood donor a couple times a year. You'll be giving the gift of life, you'll feel good about doing so, and you'll meet some great people!

537. *Intentionally learn* the fundamental lessons of business dining etiquette. These lessons are fairly simple and important to know for many reasons. There are lots of online resources and videos that you can use and if you want to have fun doing it, do it with a family member, coworker, or friend.

Now for the hard part—remember to *apply* the fundamental lessons of business dining etiquette when dining at work-related functions.

538. As a general rule, do not drink alcohol at professional business engagements. Remember drinking alcohol at any organizational function can cause unanticipated and unpredictable problems.

   Research clearly shows that alcohol usage is correlated with loss of clear thinking, emotional unintelligence, and decline in situational awareness, which can have catastrophic ramifications on one's career. So, *think before you drink!*

539. When eating out on the organization's dime, make it a priority to eat healthy: salads, fish, fruit, etc. It's just a good and easy habit!

540. Set two alarm clocks when you can't afford to miss or be late for a big trip, appointment, meeting, or presentation.

541. To be inspired and to lift your spirits, watch the 1981 movie *Chariots of Fire* which tells the story of the 1924 British Olympic track team and how they competed to win, but did so with honor! Lesson: Your faith can play a significant role in your ability to compete and be truly successful in the workplace!

542. From time to time, ask yourself the question:

   "What do my work behaviors and habits say about me as a person?"

543. Work to maintain balance in every area of your life because to not do so is to create problems for yourself and the people around you who really need you!

544. When a meeting or seminar is over, make it a habit to be the person who cleans up the mess in the room whether you helped make it or not (and don't make a big deal out of it).

545. Always stay calm in a crisis so you can think clearly and be a good example to others of "grace under fire." Just like a panic, calm in a crisis can also be contagious!

546. Be careful not to get sucked into fires that break out at work—especially ones that you didn't start!

547. Carry business cards at all times. You never know when opportunities will present themselves.

548. Don't be known as a person who takes long lunches, stretch breaks, and/or spends a lot of time hanging around the coffee station.

549. Know that profanity, vulgarity, and swearing reflects very poorly on you regardless of your organization's culture.

550. "The finest steel has to go through the hottest fire."
-Richard M. Nixon

551. Work hard to use your vacation days strategically! You deserve it!

552. Use your strategic planning skills in using your vacation time and consider three-day weekends or

taking a workday off to actually get some rest or get caught up at home.

553. Sit down with your spouse or significant other for 15 minutes at the start of each week to get your calendars synchronized! It will make for a better week, especially if you have busy professional schedules!

Getting your calendars synchronized will become even more critical if you have children, and they get older and more involved outside of your home. This practice that encourages effective communication and planning will make for a better life—and that is priceless!

554. Never allow your success to lead to arrogance, egocentrism, or hubris, which can only poison your ability to listen effectively, make wise decisions, and build great working relationships with the people you need to effectively perform your job!

555. "Humility is the true key to success. Successful people lose their way at times. They often embrace and overindulge in the fruits of success. Humility halts this arrogance and self-indulging trap. Humble people share the credit and wealth, remaining focused and hungry to continue the journey of success." -Coach Rick Pitino

556. Just a friendly reminder:
Life is tough, but it's tougher when you do stupid things!

557. Plan and manage your time so that your family is not given "the physical and emotional crumbs of your life" that are leftover from all the other things going on in your life.

558. Know and understand how your organization's financial performance impacts your 401(k)!

559. Always dress appropriately for the situation that you find yourself in at work. And if you're not sure how to dress when going into a new situation, don't be afraid to ask.

560. Be known as a person who asks good and intelligent questions in meetings.

561. Be known as a person who knows how to run great meetings.

562. Be known as a person who knows how to make interactive, effective, and dynamic presentations.

563. Always know the actual pay range for your current position as well as the positions you aspire to. There are lots of national resources online as well as regional resources that can give you an accurate picture of where you stand.

564. Don't dwell on how much more other people make compared to your own salary. That's a surefire way to feel frustrated and put yourself in a bad mood—and it changes nothing.

565. Work real hard to limit your "normal workweek" to 50 hours and don't allow working weekends to become a habit or part of your lifestyle.

566. Learn how to laugh at yourself.

567. Be confident enough to say, "I don't know, when you don't know."

568. But be smart enough to also say, "But I'll know by tomorrow"—and then know by tomorrow.

569. Keep a toothbrush, toothpaste, and mouthwash in your desk at work. The people that you work with will thank you for it!

570. Always have a good, clean, appropriate joke on the tip of your tongue to be used to illustrate a point or to lighten up a stressful situation.

571. Real attention to detail is necessary for success in most careers. (So don't make the excuse, "I am a big-picture person" when missing details or making mistakes.)

572. The emergency room is not the place to be reading your organization's health benefits plan for the first time!

Take the time to proactively know and understand this important document. In fact, go one step further and set up an appointment with a person in your organization responsible for benefits to proactively discuss the strengths and weaknesses of your coverage. And it never hurts to have your significant other attend this important meeting.

573. ## Don't be satisfied with mediocre personal performance... know that you are better than that.

574. Take the time to read your organization's annual report from cover to cover.

575. Bring donuts, bagels, or cookies to work several times a year for no particular reason—it creates goodwill.

576. Anything worth doing is worth doing not just well, but with excellence!

577. Don't waste time and create frustration "trolling" or fighting for a parking place up close to your place of employment. Just park where you can and learn to enjoy the walk. You'll be healthier for it both mentally and physically.

578. When interviewing for a new position, always ask what the previous incumbents are doing now.

579. Don't get in the habit of coming to work or meetings late because it is rude, unprofessional, and people do notice! There is no substitute for being a punctual person in all of your affairs because it speaks volumes about you.

580. ## Do not always equate the size of someone's office with the quality of his or her character or performance.

581. Take RSVP due dates seriously as it is discourteous and problematic to not do so!

582. Work hard to limit the influence of "political factors" in all personnel decisions.

583. Remember political activity creates a culture of gamesmanship and bias that discourages people, distracts people from getting work done, and ultimately creates a workplace that is perceived as being unfair.

584. If your conscience says, "Don't do it" you need to listen and listen well!

585. Your word is critically important to your creditability. So never say, "Let's get together," "I'll get back to you," "How about lunch sometime?" or "Let me look into that," without writing it down, dating it, and **following-up**! To speak these words and not take action with them causes people to not take your word seriously, and without even really intending to do so, you damage your credibility.

586. Where new job opportunities are concerned, never say no without doing some homework. Keep your options open!

587. Always keep your website up to date.

588. Get in the habit of using the steps at work. The exercise will do you good.

589. Get a physical once a year.

590. Get in the habit of taking vitamins that are age and gender appropriate.

591. If humanly possible, have lunch with your children at their school at least once a year (after getting permission from the teacher/principal).

592. Be a person who can always be trusted with confidential information, handling money, and making visitors and new employees feel welcome.

593. **Always know and completely understand your organization's active-shooter evacuation plan.** An ounce of prevention is worth a pound of cure in this context!

594. When giving a professional presentation, dress a notch more formal than those who are in attendance.

595. Never deliver any presentation without engaging your audience in some way, shape, or form!

596. Reduce your daily stress by learning how to actually operate and fix paper jams in your organization's copy machines. Know that you will be in the popular minority and that you will make new friends and confidants at work because of this talent.

597. Never underestimate the power of having a great metaphor or story to illustrate a key point during a presentation!

598. Never act like work rules or policies are somehow beneath you or only apply to others regardless of your position or level in your enterprise.

599. Be willing to admit it when you have made a mistake.

600. Keep a couple of family pictures at work and keep them up to date. It reminds people that you have a life outside of work.

601. "Honesty is the first chapter of the book of wisdom."
-Thomas Jefferson

602. Accept responsibility for your failures and share credit on all successes.

603. "Those who feel satisfied with their personal lives are more satisfied with their careers and perform better."
-Michael Hyatt

604. Important Thought: In God we trust; all others bring data!

605. Use breath mints before one-on-one meetings.

606. The ability to effectively make important decisions is a cornerstone for high performance and career success. So don't make important decisions in haste, when you're in a bad mood, when you're in an extremely good mood, without the input of informed others, and without data and/or analysis!

607. When things are not going well and you've been chastised or reprimanded, don't "dump your bucket" of frustration on those around you . . . it will only make things worse.

608. Keep a supply of Band-Aids, aspirin, mints, tissues, and cough drops at work. You never know when you will need them or when you might be able to help out a coworker.

609. Use the words *us, we,* and *our* a lot! Use the words *I, me,* and *my* infrequently and very carefully.

610. Make coffee when you take the last cup from an office communal coffeepot. Even when you're in a rush.

611. Look for job possibilities with international opportunities that can help you expand your horizons and increase your talents without compromising the needs of your family. Yes, these opportunities do exist, and it almost always takes a great deal of time and effort to secure them, but it is worth the effort!

612. Do your level best to NOT be in a hurry when . . .
    ✓ Handling money
    ✓ Giving directions to someone about how to perform an important task
    ✓ Signing a contract
    ✓ Going downstairs
    ✓ Eating, because actually chewing your food is important for your digestive health
    ✓ Listening to a customer about a problem they are having or something they consider to be important
    ✓ Interacting with an IT professional
    ✓ Engaging in any part of the hiring process, as you will have to live with the unpredictable consequences of a bad decision

613. Be strong enough to **always** tell the truth.

614. Don't run with scissors at work or at home or anywhere for that matter!

615. Always say *please*—ALWAYS!

616. Always say *thank you*—ALWAYS!

617. In the case of contract compliance, ignorance is definitely not bliss.

If your enterprise is unionized, take the time to know the labor contract and know it well. Remember, the devil is always in the details. It never hurts to sit down with your Labor Relations personnel to have them answer your questions and identify specific stress points that are tied to your specific position in the organization.

618. If your enterprise is unionized, make it a real priority to have a strong working relationship with your union stewards and president.

619. Occasionally bring healthy snacks to work to share with others in lieu of donuts and junk food.

620. Remember: crude, rude, and inappropriate language is a window to your heart, so let your language reflect your integrity and character!

621. **Remember also: crude, rude, and inappropriate language is always going to offend some people, so let your language reflect your concern for everyone!**

622. Remember finally: crude, rude, and inappropriate language has no place in front of your customers, as you are a representative and ambassador of your organization!

623. It's well worth repeating: "Life and death are in the power of the tongue."

624. Keep your shoes shined.

625. Be confident enough to wear fun socks to work!

626. Remember to turn off your ringer on your cell phone in meetings, seminars, and training programs.

627. When in an important meeting or training program, shut your cell phone off altogether (and let others see you doing it). It sends a number of powerful messages to those in charge of the gathering and those around you!

628. ## Work hard to be the "kindest" person your coworkers and friends know.

629. "I keep six honest serving men: they taught me all I knew: their names are What and Why and When and How and Where and Who." -Rudyard Kipling

630. Always keep your expense account paperwork up to date. Remember the time value of money.

631. ## Remember that your smart phone is great a tool to help you increase your personal effectiveness and keep you connected. But it is not something to be worshiped or controlled by!

632. When spending your organization's money, only buy "things" in airports in an emergency.

633. "What people don't realize is that professionals are sensational because of the fundamentals. The sensationalism has taken over the professionalism." -Barry Larkin

634. Know and understand our country's affirmative-action and workplace-discrimination laws. Take the time and effort to know and understand these important documents and guidelines which are designed to give each and every person in the workplace equal opportunity and fair treatment.

Champion these critically important issues at your place of employment and remember that actions speak louder than words!

635. Always keep real perspective on your circumstances no matter how good or bad things may be! Why? Because things are generally never as good nor as bad as they seem. Remember that we tend to overestimate how bad things really are, so keep your head!

636. Goodwill begets goodwill in almost every business situation, despite what the critics might say.

637. Plan ahead so you can take your birthday off work as a gift to yourself (and don't forget to call your mother).

638. Learn to overcome your fears in every area of your life. As a general rule, the only way to overcome your fears is to face them head-on. And remember what author Richie Norton had to say: "To escape fear, you have to go through it, not around."

So next time you're afraid to do a presentation, take a job interview, take on a new assignment, or are forced out of your comfort zone at work, be brave and push forward and you will come out on the other side at a minimum having learned a lot and at a maximum having defeated your fears! Either way you win, which is necessary for long-term career success.

639. Learn how to facilitate effective problem-solving/brainstorming sessions. This is a talent that is in great demand in the modern workplace.

640. Distractions can cause mistakes for lots of different reasons. When you need to work on truly important and/or high-profile projects, find a quiet place where you can concentrate and where you will not be disturbed. You may have to find a place to hide to accomplish this!

641. Remember that most really important decisions in modern organizations are rarely made by committees or by voting.

642. Know and understand the causes and symptoms of poor customer service. And when your organization's customer service levels are not where they need to be, be the champion that tries to improve them!

643. Be reminded that when one of your customers has a poor experience they will typically share their experience with at least nine other people by word-of-mouth. And if it's a really bad customer experience, they just might take it to cyberspace with the goal of sharing it with everyone on planet Earth.

Lesson: Real professionals have every incentive to take great care of their customers, especially when there is a problem!

644. Always carry a pen/pencil with you—even with all the technology that we carry!

645. Proactively take the time to keep your spouse or significant other informed about what is going on at work. They generally want to know and will then be in a better position to understand what you're up against and how to best assist you!

646. "I hope I shall possess firmness and virtue enough to maintain what I consider the most enviable of all titles, the character of an honest man." -George Washington

647. Losing your job is not the end of the world. Analyze why it happened, understand the real causes, and develop a plan to secure a job that builds on your strengths! Our research with high-performance business leaders shows that the majority of them have experienced being downsized, demoted, or terminated at some point during their careers.

It is important to note that these successful people used their temporary setback as a catalyst for major positive changes in their professional and personal lives! So when experiencing this type of setback, know that you're not alone, and that it is imperative to get up, dust yourself off, learn from the experience, and keep moving forward! Yes, you can do this despite what your feelings might be telling you!

648. Never talk about yourself in third person—it almost always comes off poorly!

649. Question: Is your life really worth a split-second distraction?
Answer: Do not text while you drive!

650. Do not text while walking through parking lots, crossing the street, walking on steps, or sitting in a meeting. All can have very bad outcomes!

651. Be brave and smart enough to always do the right thing. And take the time to share your stories of doing so with your children.

652. Your character and integrity are two of the only things in your life that you have complete control over, so guard them wisely.

653. "Integrity is telling myself the truth. And honesty is telling the truth to other people." - Spencer Johnson

654. Our modern workplace is filled with many "temptations" and yet organizations rarely if ever use the word in discussions of decision-making, ethics training and/or leadership-development programs! Consider why not.

655. Note that each and every job that you will ever have over the course of your career will have "temptations" attached to it, all of which have the power to destroy you, your career, your reputation, and your family if you fall prey to them. Please take this warning very seriously!

656. Understand the definition of the word *temptation* (temp-ta-tion) *n*: a desire for something bad or unacceptable; a craving for something considered wrong; the stimulation of desire or yearning for something usually considered to be wrong.

657. Know that no one sets out to be an ethical failure at work! Ethical failure is a choice driven by ineffective, clouded, and poor decision-making! And getting caught up in an unethical, illegal, or immoral situation at work does not happen without a person making a conscious decision that was not right.

658. Our research shows that a person's organizational success can actually set the table for ethical failure! Success can bring with it:
   ✓ Bigger titles and better rewards
   ✓ Greater status and influence
   ✓ Greater control over organizational resources
   ✓ Increased access
   ✓ Less direct supervision and accountability for daily actions

- ✓ Greater control over decision-making
- ✓ An inflated ego
- ✓ Fewer real friends
- ✓ No work/life balance
- ✓ A mindset of self-gratification

When taken together, these organizational realities associated with success can actually open the door for ethical temptation and devastating failure. And we read about it every day in the newspapers when good and principled people, in all walks of life, make unethical, illegal, and immoral decisions because of their inability to handle their success!

659. FACT: Organizations are quick to tell their people what **not** to do, but rarely give them the **tools** to conquer the temptations that come with the territory.

To be truly successful in building your career, you must create your own "ethical tool kit" and you must be reminded that each and every new position you take on will have its own unique set of ethical and moral temptations that you must contend with to remain both successful and a person of character.

660. When making *any* business decision, determine the extent to which ethical/moral issues might be at play.

661. When facing an ethical decision-making dilemma at work, it is important to recognize that the decision you are struggling with may have already been made for you, so check out your organization's . . .
- Policy and procedure manual
- Rules and regulations
- Union contract
- Code of conduct

Make sure that you're not wasting time, effort, and energy on a decision that has already been made by your enterprise. Then, once you realize that this decision has been made for you, not following it puts you right back in the middle of a new ethical dilemma of your own making!

662. Know that the presence of ethical/moral dilemmas embedded in any business decision require more information and facts, greater analysis, and greater input and counsel from others! Before you step into the street when making a decision with ethical/moral implications, make sure that you look both ways, hold hands tightly, and step into the street together as a decision-making team. There is always wisdom, safety, and security in numbers.

663. When facing an ethical decision-making dilemma, ask the following critically important questions:

✓ Is this decision legal?

- ✓ Is this decision in line with my organization's values?
- ✓ Is this decision in line with my own values?
- ✓ How will this decision impact the stakeholders?
- ✓ What is the upside of this decision?
- ✓ What is the downside of this decision?
- ✓ What would our Board of Directors think about this decision?
- ✓ Would I be comfortable having this decision circulated in the company newsletter?
- ✓ What would my mom think about this decision?

664. Know that far too many ethical failings in the workplace happen because people do not think through the long-term ramifications of their decisions. Serious decision-making rarely if ever takes place in a vacuum, unobserved, all without leaving an electronic or paper trail. This is an important exercise to get in the habit of: Before making any important ethical decision, ask and answer the following question:

"What are the long-term ramifications of making this decision on my character, career, organization, livelihood, and family?"

An honest answer to this question just might steer you away from making a bad decision with harmful and unpredictable consequences!

665. Know that far too many catastrophic ethical failures have nothing to do with business decision-making; rather they focus on unethical personal decision-making for personal gain and/or pleasure!

666. So take the time to identify the ethical and moral challenges and temptations that are attached to your current position at work. Answer the following question for yourself: "What are the ethical and moral temptations associated with the position that I currently hold?"

Take the time to make a list of these ethical/moral challenges that confront you because of the position that you hold.

Once you have identified the ethical challenges you face, you will be in a position to prepare yourself to defeat them in battle!

667. Our research shows reoccurring themes of ethical and moral temptation that cut across virtually every discipline, organizational level, and every type of enterprise. From one of our recent studies, here is the top 10 list of temptations confronting leaders:

- ✓ Misuse of authority and power for personal gain
- ✓ Falsifying and/or misusing organizational information
- ✓ Inappropriate sexual relationships
- ✓ Knowingly violating organizational policy for personal gain
- ✓ Offering and/or accepting bribes or special favors
- ✓ Drug and alcohol abuse in the workplace
- ✓ Workplace favoritism
- ✓ Turning a "blind eye" to organizational wrongdoing

✓ Financial wrongdoing
✓ Misuse of organizational resources for personal gain

Which of the temptations on this list confront you? Identify them and prepare yourself to effectively respond!

668. Good people are always quick to say, "It could never happen to me!" or "I am better than that!" . . . Virtually every good person that has ever been caught up in a significant ethical failure has made the same statement.

    Don't kid yourself! Without preparation, discipline, and due diligence, all of us could potentially fall prey to an ethical failure brought on by our workplace situation, our success, and our personal vulnerabilities. The good news is you know how to prepare for battle, so read on!

669. Once you've identified the temptations you face, proactively conduct an ethical/moral SWOT Analysis on yourself to see how you stack up against the temptations that come with your current position and carefully answer the following questions:

    ✓ What are your ethical/moral **strengths** and how can they help you deal with the temptations attached to your current position?

✓ What are your ethical/moral **weaknesses** at this point of your life and how might they create vulnerabilities for you in your current position?

✓ What are the **opportunities** that exist for wrongdoing created by your current position and organizational culture?

✓ What are the ethical/moral **threats** that can potentially erode your character in your current work situation?

670. Always take the time to carefully read, assess, and understand your organization's Code of Conduct. This is also a great exercise to go through with your peers and/or coworkers in your organization so that you are in a position to create peer accountability around the code.

671. Once you know and understand your organization's Code of Conduct, create your own "Personal Code of Conduct" that clearly articulates what you absolutely stand for and which addresses your current work-related temptations and challenges.

672. Put your Personal Code of Conduct in writing and post it in a special place that will frequently remind you of the ethical/moral standard that you are committed to. Even consider sharing it with your spouse and with your children! This lets them know how seriously you take your role and sets a great example for those who truly depend on you.

673. Create a personal mantra that clearly articulates in a single phrase what you stand for and your greater

purpose in life. When confronted with temptation, use your mantra to help you stay focused on your higher calling!

Mantras of note that have emerged in our senior leader research:

- ✓ "I will always do the right thing!"
- ✓ "What would I do if my kids were here?"
- ✓ "Think, and then think again!"
- ✓ "What would my spouse say?"
- ✓ "Does this decision support my noble calling as a leader?"
- ✓ "Stay strong and avoid wrong."
- ✓ "Always look for the way of escape."
- ✓ "Remember my noble calling!"
- ✓ "Be good, stay good, do good."
- ✓ "What would my mother do if she caught me doing this?"
- ✓ "Am I better than this decision that I am making?"

674. Get and keep your ethical guardrails up!

Your personal ethical guardrails are specific practices/safeguards designed by you to prevent you from "going over the edge" and making unethical/immoral/illegal decisions that might cost you your job, career, reputation, family, and livelihood!

675. In one of our recent studies we asked a large group of senior leaders to build out a set of guardrails that they believe would be useful to help keep business leaders doing the right things. Here are a few of their recommendations:

- ✓ Develop a relationship with an accountability partner with whom you meet regularly.
- ✓ Take time for personal reflection to increase your self-awareness of what you are doing and why you are doing it.
- ✓ Practice servant leadership to maintain humility and to remind yourself that you are at work to serve others.
- ✓ Develop specific safeguards around any area you deem to be a vulnerability.
- ✓ Seek out input from organizational/industry experts when unsure of appropriate actions.
- ✓ Increase your situational awareness of potential threats.
- ✓ Establish and maintain consistent and transparent communications with the people around you at work.
- ✓ Develop your faith and spirituality to recognize your higher calling.
- ✓ Make use of third parties and establish procedures in situations involving money, outside vendors, and resource allocation.
- ✓ Make use of organizational safeguards that are already in place which are designed to protect you.

The important point in this discussion is to build safeguards into your business activity to prevent you from facing potential temptations that you just might fall prey to.

676. Always remember this critical key point: **It is easier to avoid temptation than to resist temptation!**

677. Use your temptation map and your "situational awareness" to help you stay out of potentially troublesome ethical situations! Do not knowingly walk into situations where you know you will be vulnerable! Remember the military axiom, "Forewarned is forearmed!"

678. Create accountability with a person (or people) strong and honest enough to be your mentor, accountability partner, and watchdog, who knows what you're up against in the workplace and can help you deal with these issues.

When confronted with an ethical temptation or moral trial, immediately tell a confidant that you trust and seek out their assessment, input, guidance, and support. We are all less likely to do wrongful things when we know that others know! This accountability is priceless!

679. Remember that because you are operating in the "information age," there's a very good chance that you will be found out for any questionable decisions you make!

680. Practice staying **focused** and **humble** by being a servant leader and regularly doing some of the lowliest jobs in your operation. This will send the powerful message to the people around you that your feet are planted firmly on the ground!

681. For a striking mini case study in major-league ethical failure by a great and principled

leader, read the account of King David and Bathsheba in II Samuel 11 and see what you learn! One unethical/immoral decision by the good King David led to a chain reaction of big-time, life-changing trouble!

682. If your boss asks you to do something that you know is wrong, ask them to explain why they are asking you to do something that they know is wrong!

683. If your boss asks you to do something that you know is wrong, seek the input and counsel of someone you know and respect to help you find the best way to do the right thing.

684. If your boss asks you to do something that you know is wrong, ask them to put it in writing!

685. If your boss asks you to do something that you know is wrong, employ the Nike slogan in reverse—just don't do it!

686. Always tell the truth, as one lie leads to another and the cycle can be endless with horrible, unforeseen consequences.

687. Learn to pace yourself! Life is not a sprint but rather a marathon.

688. If at all humanly possible, do not take work on vacation with you. You truly deserve and need time to renew!

689. Start each day by counting your personal and professional blessings! We all have much to be thankful for but sometimes lose sight of that fact in our rush to do life! Engaging in this practice will put you in a better mood to start your day.

690. Always keep confidential information confidential.

691. Remember that jealousy and selfish ambition can suck the joy from your work and life.

692. Keep your watch set three minutes ahead and forget about it.

693. Remember that how you handle stress speaks volumes to others about who you really are.

694. Be willing, prepared, and strong enough to take educated/calculated risks. Risk-taking is required for a successful career!

695. Know and understand what portion of your contribution to your 401(k) goes into your own organization's stock.

696. Much of the stigma associated with "job jumping" every couple years has dissipated. But be careful not to develop a reputation as a person who changes jobs without reason, closure, or leaving on good terms with their previous employer! People do talk and share information!

697. Important counsel: Be confident enough to negotiate for your salary going *into* a new position because once you accept an offer, your leverage is gone.

It is imperative that you do your homework and obtain a realistic analysis of what the job is worth in your region for an organization of similar size. When given a job offer, know this simple fact—employers generally make their first offer at the low end of the salary range for that position! In their mind, it's just good business to start low.

When a salary offer is made, respond using this statement, "Thank you for this offer. I'm excited to work for this organization and know that I will do a good job for you—no, I will do a *great* job for you. But I was thinking more along the lines of . . . (inflate the offer by at least 10%)."
—and then shut your mouth!

When making a counter-offer, there is a tendency to blather and ramble about why you are asking for more money. Don't do it—it's not your employer's business. Keep your mouth shut! Don't be surprised if the person you are talking to who is representing the organization gasps or recoils but this is just a business transaction, so stay calm, and keep your mouth shut

698. Practice this negotiation technique so you can come off with great confidence and know that if an employer has made you an offer, they are not going to pull it because of your conscientious request.

699. Accept positions you are truly excited about and do not

second-guess yourself once you are on the job.

700. When making a decision about taking a job, always assess the quality of the people that you'll be working with and your potential boss's track record for developing people and building teams!

701. Know that the best motivational practices are the ones that work.

702. Allow yourself time to "catch your breath" between meetings and appointments.

703. Don't let your work success cause you to make unwise personal financial decisions.

704. Stand tall, at all times! Your posture is a powerful nonverbal to others.

705. Take the time to read Stephen Covey's classic, *The 7 Habits of Highly Effective People*, as it will reinforce and underscore some of the more important things you have read in this book!

706. "Leadership is a potent combination of strategy and character. But if you must be without one, be without the strategy." -General Norman Schwarzkopf

707. **Whatever you are doing, always do your best to finish STRONG!**

EPILOGUE
A Call for Action!

"Life is tough, but it's tougher if you are stupid!" – John Wayne

"The challenges of life mandate that we apply all our wisdom to daily situations lest we fall prey to our own folly." -Socrates

Thank you for reading the lengthy collection of ideas, concepts, and practices that are contained in this book. While I'm confident that a great deal of this information resonated with you, we need to remember the words of Thomas Edison: ***"The value of an idea lies in using it."*** So let me ask you an important question:

What specific ideas in this book resonated with you and what are you going to do to implement them into your life?

Before I offer you some specific counsel about how to do this, I want to make a couple important points about adult learning that are critically important for your future success.

Let me start by asking you to conduct the **Career Success and Survival Assessment** for a second time and see what happens to your scores on each of the key Career Imperatives. If you are like most people, your scores will go down! The reason for this is that you now hopefully have a better picture of what each of these 12 Career Imperatives looks like in operation in the workplace, and so you can rate yourself more accurately equipped with the knowledge you now have.

Carefully read each question and rate yourself using the following scale to determine where you stand on each imperative:

1 = I am clearly failing at this imperative
2 = I am really struggling with this imperative
3 = I am barely adequate with this imperative
4 = I am good with this imperative
5 = I am exceptional with this imperative

1. I consistently identify and deliver the value-added <u>desired results</u> my organization wants and needs from me on an ongoing basis. _____

2. I recognize, implement, and stay focused on the key value-added <u>practices/behaviors</u> that lead to desired results on an ongoing basis. _____

3. I focus my <u>time,</u> <u>organizational resources,</u> and <u>power</u> on delivering desired results. _____

4. I forge and foster viable, effective <u>working relationships</u> and <u>business networks</u> with the people I need to get desired results. _____

5. I effectively <u>communicate</u> and <u>connect with</u> everyone in every situation at work. _____

6. I work to maintain and project a positive <u>personality,</u> <u>attitude,</u> and <u>outlook</u> about myself, my work, and my life. _____

7. I maintain my "<u>situational awareness</u>" so that I always <u>know what is going on</u> around me and <u>how well</u> I am actually performing. _____

8. I continually <u>learn</u> and <u>develop</u> the <u>skills/talents</u> necessary to meet the changing demands of my job. _____

9. I embrace <u>feedback</u> and <u>coaching</u> and seek out <u>accountability</u> for improvement. _____

10. I work hard to be a disciplined <u>problem-solver</u> and <u>change agent</u> to make it easier to get things done. _____

11. I effectively <u>handle stress</u>, <u>stay poised</u>, and <u>maintain balance</u> in every area of my personal and professional life. _____

12. I demonstrate <u>character</u> and <u>integrity</u> in all of my personal and professional dealings. _____

SCORING: In the space provided below please write down your score for each of these 12 questions and fill out the subtotal for each section. When that is complete, add up your four subtotal scores and determine your **GRAND TOTAL.**

Ongoing Focus and Alignment

Question #1: _____

Question #2: _____

Question #3: _____

SUBTOTAL: _____

Creating Real People Power

Question #4: _____

Question #5: _____

Question #6: _____

SUBTOTAL: _____

Ongoing Learning and Performance Improvement

Question #7: _____

Question #8: _____

Question #9: _____

Question #10: _____

SUBTOTAL: _____

True Grit Professionalism and Character

Question #11: _____

Question #12: _____

SUBTOTAL: _____

GRAND TOTAL (all four sections): _____

Use the following scoring key a second time to determine where you stand based on your assessment of yourself.

Score 12–23: Career Danger Zone

Score 24–35: Career Success Improvement Required

Score 36–47: Career Strengths Are Emerging

Score 48–60: Career Strengths Are in Place

So here's the BIG question: What have you learned about your career strengths and opportunities for improvement and what actions do you need to take to bring your career to the next level? Your response to this question is truly important, and for most of us, it requires some degree of change, which can be a real challenge.

I have found time and time again in my consulting, research, executive coaching, and management-development programs around the world that real change is difficult for most of us. This is especially true when we are exceptionally busy or when we take a "business as usual" approach. I have witnessed people walk out of great learning experiences with useful and game-changing information that could make a real difference in their careers and lives. But they went right back to business as usual, throwing away the opportunity to improve their workplace performance and career opportunities. This happens because the information they were exposed to was never properly internalized, applied, or implemented, so it simply fell by the wayside and provided the recipient with little or no return on their investment.

Without a game plan for real implementation, good career and development information by itself is fairly worthless. While the information might be good, true, make sense, make you think, and might hold the *potential* to make a real difference in your career, it is just INFORMATION!

I want you to carefully re-read the quote at the start of this section from Socrates and the words often attributed to the great American film actor John Wayne. Socrates states very clearly that if we do not apply wisdom, things that we know are good and true, we will fall prey to our own folly—or *foolishness*. And while Socrates is an intellectual and philosophical powerhouse, I personally prefer the saying we often attribute to John Wayne, which is basically the same thing. An ignorant person does not know what to do in a given situation, so they can get training, read a book, go online, seek out help from a co-worker or mentor, or engage in any number of practices that will allow them to get their hands on what they need to know. But always remember we are being stupid when we *know* what to do and for whatever reason we choose not to do it—making life more difficult for ourselves. In a nutshell, the key here is to be WISE. And we know that wise people learn what to do and find ways to apply good information and wisdom to their daily lives! That's why "real learning" is so critical to this wrap-up discussion.

We have found that good and useful information has to be taken through a learning process by an adult learner to create real value. In fact, we have found that powerful and useful information without MOTIVATION on the part of the recipient typically goes *nowhere* without special attention. Real motivation means that an adult learner has an inner drive, a passion, a hunger, and a real commitment to acting on ideas, concepts, and practices because they consider them to be truly important!

So get out your **Career Imperative Note Sheet** of the things you highlighted while going through the book and answer the following questions for yourself:

✓ What lessons have I learned in this book that I am truly excited about?

✓ What lessons and ideas do I have a real desire to implement?

✓ What practices do I truly aspire to make part of my daily approach to work and life?

Without this motivation which is the starting point for real learning, there's a good chance that you will not make any real changes in your approach to work and life.

We have also found that when an adult learner has both good information and strong motivation to put that information into action, it is critically important that they fully engage in the process of INTEGRATION. Integration means that an idea, concept, or practice is thoroughly known and understood by the learner. Full integration means you have taken the time to master and develop a full knowledge of a particular idea, concept, or practice so that it becomes part of the your intellectual and emotional

DNA. To get at integration requires an individual to be able to answer the following questions:

- ✓ Do I have a strong understanding of why this idea, concept, or practice is truly important to me in my career and personal success?
- ✓ Do I have a full understanding of how to engage and/or implement this idea, concept, or practice into my life?
- ✓ Could I explain the importance and operation of this idea, concept, or practice to another person in a fashion that makes sense?

Integration is so important because as adult learners we have to build an intellectual and emotional "bond" with the idea, concept, or practice so that we are then in a position to apply it to our daily lives. If we begin to apply without integration, in fairly short order we will backslide, drop the ball, or go back to business as usual! Integration is the cornerstone of making real change happen in our lives so we must take it very seriously!

It is then the process of APPLICATION becomes paramount, which means that we are now actively implementing specific ideas, concepts, or practices in our lives that can now be observed, monitored, measured, and coached/reinforced. When we finally take this step, we are then in a position to develop different and potentially better work and life habits. We need to be able to answer the following questions as they pertain to our ability to implement specific new behaviors and practices into our routine:

✓ Am I truly committed to doing the things necessary to make this new practice or behavior part of my regular routine, behavior, and mindset?

✓ What specific things will prevent me from properly implementing a new practice or behavior into my life or falling back to my old ways of doing things?

✓ How will I track my daily performance and who will help hold me accountable for implementing a new practice or behavior into my life?

Application is the final step to improving your career success and survival. When all these pieces of the adult learning model come together, we are in a better position to experience real change and improvement in our lives.

It is at that point that we experience what I like to call TRANSFORMATION. The meaning of the word *transformation* is important here: a thorough or dramatic change in form or appearance, also known as metamorphosis. The meaning of *metamorphosis* takes this understanding to an even higher level as it is the process of great, sudden, and dramatic change in a person's form, thought, behavior, and habits. When an adult learner goes through transformation, it means that you are a different person from who you were when you started—which should be the goal of any important learning experience! Ongoing transformation is what allows us to keep aligned with the rapidly changing world. Rapid transformation is what allows us to develop a competitive advantage in the workplace. And ongoing transformation is the process that can take us from GOOD to GREAT!

So let's go back to Pat, the struggling business leader with whom we opened this book. As you may remember, Pat had had a discussion with his boss that had shaken him to his core. He was told he was not developing as a leader and that he was not delivering the desired results that were needed for him and his team to be successful.

I had given Pat an assignment to have a Personal Strategic Planning Retreat with himself and I emailed him 12 questions that I knew he needed to answer before we met to discuss developing his Personal Performance Improvement Plan. The 12 questions Pat needed to answer were those associated with the 12 Career Success and Survival Imperatives that we have discussed throughout the course of this book. So Pat had a two-hour meeting with himself, an important beginning for him to do some serious soul-searching about improving his performance and getting his career back on track. That meeting has become such a turning point in his life that he now refers to it simply as "my morning at the park."

When Pat and I met the following Tuesday, I asked him to make a presentation to me and summarize what he learned about himself during his "morning at the park." I must state for the record that he was an excellent student in that he took my homework assignment very seriously. Here is a summary of the actual notes that he shared. I strongly believe that you will be able to relate to the challenges that he faced and some of the conclusions that he has drawn:

1. While I thought my boss and I were on the same page, we are not, and that's on me—I need to identify exactly the results we need to achieve the next two quarters for myself and for my operation as a whole. I think we are pursuing too many things

and we are not on the same page, which is also on me. We/I need better focus and prioritization of what we need to accomplish and I have got to become more effective at doing so.

2. I need to spend more time on high-value activities and investing in my people. I need to spend less time in meetings and on paperwork and more time working with key people. Also, I need to learn how to say no as I have been getting involved with too many things that are not part of my core responsibilities.

3. I am not a good steward of my time and I spread myself too thin. I could make better use of my time and organizational resources, but I don't plan as effectively as I need to which means I get caught by both surprises and sometimes fires of my own making. I think I have the resources that I need but I'm not using them in an optimal fashion because I don't take time to think as deeply as I should. I know that I need to delegate more effectively—some of the things I'm caught up in could be delegated to some of my direct reports and it would both help them develop and free up my time for more important issues.

4. I have been so busy and running so hard lately that I have ignored or failed to invest in and build relationships with my people. As a general rule, I like people and I enjoy building teams and coaching people. But I need to spend more time one-on-one with my direct reports and better build and invest in these important relationships. I also have a couple people on

my staff that I do not know very well and I need to make getting to know them a priority right now.

5. While I have a pretty good network of people in the organization, I don't know if I listen as well as I should to the things going on in our operation. I do try to share information, but I don't always know if I'm getting through. I need to set up a better and more systematic approach to communicating with people in my operation, and I think I need to schedule some formal "listening sessions" to get my arms around if I am keeping people and myself informed about what is going on.

6. I know that sometimes, when I'm moving real fast—which seems to be all the time—I can get short with people and at times project a negative attitude, which is not reflective of who I really am. I need to become more of a "cheerleader" for my people and for our operation. I was thinking about something that happened several weeks ago when I said something sarcastic to one of my people that was not well received. I was just trying to be funny but I need to be more sensitive to this issue which seems to have crept into how I interact with some of my people which is not good. I don't know where this has come from but I do not want to be known as someone who is sarcastic or cynical.

7. Obviously my situational awareness is not where it needs to be or I would not have been caught off guard by my meeting with the president last week. I need to spend more time tracking where my time is going and what I'm working on. I need to spend time each day reflecting on where things are at, where

my time is going, and how I invest each day. I need to pay better attention to our key performance metrics as a whole. I have a couple that I track very carefully, but I need to look at the whole performance picture more frequently so I am in a better position to make ongoing adjustments.

8. While I read a lot, I do not have a tangible performance-improvement plan. Conducting this personal retreat helped me identify some things that really need some work. When I took on this new position I don't know if I ever clearly identified the specific talents that I needed to improve upon to make the jump to the next level. I am going to put together a list of 3 to 5 things and target them for the next 30 days. Time management is going to be at the head of the list.

9. With the exception of my wife, I receive very little feedback or coaching from anyone. The president of our company is not real big on coaching. He lets people do their own thing. That is not a good thing for me and I need to build in some structured feedback and accountability from some people that I trust. While I do have a couple of people that I consider to be mentors, I do not have any kind of accountability for my personal performance. I need to get on that ASAP.

10. I do believe that I am good at helping people in my operation solve their problems and improve their processes but I don't know if I would describe myself as a change agent. I typically think tactically and not strategically and we have some significant changes to be made that fall into the strategic category. I need to allocate more of my time to help my people

operate more efficiently and remove roadblocks. I don't think of myself as being a change agent but maybe I need to start doing so! I think that I can lead the changes that we need to make but I need to stay focused to do so.

11. I think that I handle stress pretty well but I think everybody thinks that when you're in a leadership position. The fact that my attitude goes dark sometimes suggests otherwise. In terms of balance, I am not in a good place as I put in too much time at work, which takes me away from other things that I consider to be important. My family and my health deserve more time and I want to become more balanced. The fact that I'm in trouble with my boss right now makes me want me to jump in and devote more time to work but I do need to work more efficiently on the activities that will make the biggest difference. That way maybe I can free up more time for these other very important things. I am passionate about what I do and I like to work hard so I need to get my arms around the questions that have already been discussed if I'm going to get any balance in my life.

12. Of all the things that you asked me to think about, this is the one that I can give myself high marks on because I do have a personal code of conduct that I live by, and I work very hard to demonstrate character and integrity in everything I do! And while this was the last question on your list, it is number one on my list because it is critically important to me. I try to encourage my people to always demonstrate their character and integrity, and I try hard to be a role model to them in this

regard. So while I wasn't feeling great about most of these questions, I feel like I ended up on a high note.

When Pat finished sharing his "morning at the park" assessment of himself against the 12 Career Success and Survival Imperatives that I had asked him to complete, I simply said, "Wow. Thanks for taking this assignment seriously and for your candor in doing so. You have just taken a big first step forward to turn things around and it only cost you a couple of hours!"

Pat agreed and said, "You know what, this is something that I should do once a month because it was very helpful. I enjoyed taking the time to think through these issues. I know I've got my work cut out for me, but I know that these are all things that I can do."

This was breakthrough thinking for Pat, and we ended up spending about 90 minutes fleshing out a pretty comprehensive personal performance-improvement plan that Pat implemented with great vigor over the course of the next six months. Did Pat's performance improve? Absolutely. There were still some bumps in the road for him but he had created a process to improve himself on an ongoing basis, and most importantly, he *owned* his improvement plan!

Pat figured out what he needed to do to create transformation in his work and personal life so that he was in a better position to make a real difference and I'm confident that you can do the same. So now let's talk about how to make that happen in your life, using the same approach that I used with Pat and hundreds of people that I have coached on their road to career success.

A TIME FOR ACTION

Let me put on my coaching hat and offer you some very unambiguous counsel about the specific things that you can do to drive transformation in your professional and personal life. While many of the ideas that we are about to discuss are already contained in the book, this discussion will give you a framework within which to apply the specific ideas, concepts, and practices that you believe can help you improve. Let's approach this discussion as if you are a "business unit of one person" who wants to take your business to the next level of success. We know that successful organizations always have a clear mission/purpose, a strong and distinguishing strategy, and the ability to execute specific tactics on a daily basis that will allow them to separate themselves from their competitors. That's how I would like you to think about yourself as you prepare to develop your personal performance-improvement plan. Let's get started!

Key Coaching Tip #1: Schedule a Personal Strategic Planning Retreat with Yourself and Be Prepared - Once you've completed reading this book it is important that you plan ahead and set aside 90–120 minutes for a strategic planning retreat with yourself as a business unit of one person.

Here are some important guidelines for this planning retreat: Find a time that is not "shoehorned" in between other important activities just in case it takes longer than you think. You do not want to have to disrupt your thought and planning processes if you are on a roll. Find a quiet place where you will not be disturbed—yes, they still do exist, but they are not as easy to find as they once were. And do not attempt to do this while at work. Public libraries typically have quiet spaces or individual study rooms that can be signed out. Public parks can be a great place as long as you will not be distracted by the weather or the activities going on around you. The important point is that you will find a place where you will not be distracted and that your surroundings will make it easier for you to THINK.

It's always good to turn off your cell phone and "unplug," bring a thermos of coffee/tea or a bottle of water, and wear comfortable clothes. You want to be comfortable so your thinking is not sidetracked or diverted from your mission.

Finally, it is important to get a good night's sleep before your planning retreat, which will again help you think. I can tell you with great confidence that taking this time to proactively think about and plan your professional and personal improvement is <u>priceless</u> in terms of the impact that it can have on your ability to get and stay on track. You will see, like many of my clients, that there is no substitute for this thinking time for reflection and direction.

Key Coaching Tip #2: Start Your Retreat by Clarifying Your Mission - Your first activity needs to be writing out your **personal career mission statement** about what you want to achieve with your career and how you plan on doing it. Clearly answer each of the following questions:

- ✓ What do I want to accomplish with my career in my current job?
- ✓ How will I conduct and represent myself?
- ✓ What are my priorities?
- ✓ How will I make a difference with my career?

You want to capture your response to these important questions in a statement that will help establish an "umbrella" of the key activities and practices that you want to engage in to improve your performance. Try to limit your mission statement to 2 to 4 sentences that capture who you essentially are, what you want to achieve, and how you are going to operate. Remember that the best mission statements are short, inspiring, and create great focus for action.

Do not underestimate the importance of clarifying these key principles in your mind and on paper. Just like in an organization, your mission statement should help you target your activities, allow for better planning, and help you allocate your key resources appropriately.

Key Coaching Tip #3: Needs Assessment Time to Review the Career Success and Survival Imperatives - Go back over your Career Success and Survival Assessment from the back of the book and look carefully at your strengths and opportunities for improvement. Now arrange the imperatives based on your scores from lowest to highest across all 12 dimensions of the assessment. This should give you a very good idea on how to identify opportunities for improvement. Now go to the appendix and answer each of the **12 Career Success and Survival Assessment Questions** in detail following the same order from lowest to highest. And please take the time to write out each of your responses with as much detail as possible.

When this is complete you have done a solid job of conducting a "needs assessment" on yourself in terms of identifying exact areas that just might need some specific attention while at the same time identifying areas where your performance is already solid! Once you've responded to all 12 questions individually, go back and read through them from start to finish in one reading. When you've completed this reading ask yourself the following question: **What have I learned about myself?** Now you're in a position to develop your performance-improvement action plan.

Key Coaching Tip #4: Formulate Your 90-Day Action Plan - Based on what you have learned in your assessment and review of the 12 Career Success and Survival Imperatives, it's now time as a business unit of one to make some key decisions about what you are going to do to improve your performance and keep your career moving in the right direction. Here's the good news—you've already completed your needs assessment of the areas that need improvement and you've already identified some of the specific lessons that you thought were truly important when reading this book. So get out your **Career Imperative Note Sheet** again and use it to help you write out your answers to the following three critically important questions that are going to become the basis for your Personal Performance Improvement Plan.

To improve my performance in the next 90 days, what do I need to. . .

a) *Keep Doing?* Build on your strengths and keep doing more of the things that you know are working well and making a real difference in your ability to get results for your employer. Play to your strengths and the things that you know are currently making a real difference in your ability to deliver desired results in your current position.

b) **Stop Doing?** Identify the specific things that you believe are counterproductive or are damaging your ability to get the desired results you need for success in your current position. For many people, this is a critically important dimension of their performance-improvement plan. If you've identified ineffective, counterproductive, or even destructive personal behaviors and practices that are damaging your ability to deliver desired results for your employer, you must identify what you need to stop doing and how you are going to prevent these behaviors and practices from reemerging in your work/personal life.

c) **Start Doing?** Identify the specific behaviors and practices that you need to start doing to take your game up a notch. In the context of the 12 Career Success and Survival Imperatives, what specific activities, practices, and behaviors need to be built into and expanded in your work life to improve your performance? Be as specific as possible!

In developing your Keep, Stop, and Start responses, be very specific and do not overwhelm yourself. Identify the specific behaviors and practices that you believe you will get the biggest bang for the buck in improving your performance during the next 90 days. And remember it is vitally important that you tie your response to these important questions back to the 12 Career Success and Survival Imperatives.

Key Coaching Tip #5: Present Your 90-Day Action Plan to an Accountability Partner or Your Personal Board of Directors - We know from our research that two of the primary reasons that people do not change their work behavior is because they do not have a real, well-thought-out plan to do so and/or they have little or no accountability for real action. I want to encourage you to develop your improvement plan and drill down on each of the key action items that you wish to implement in your work life. You should already have three primary categories that are part of your personal improvement plan: Keep Doing, Stop Doing, and Start Doing with specific targeted behaviors and practices in each category.

When your write-up is complete I would like you to put together a PowerPoint presentation so that you can share your plan with a person that you have identified as an accountability partner or a small group of people that you have set up to become part of your personal board of directors. It is a great practice to get three or four people together that you trust and know well to serve as board members or an advisory council to help each other go through this process together.

Find people that you know outside of work whom you respect and who have technical expertise and experience that can complement your own. Sharing your Personal Improvement Plan with others creates personal accountability and opens the door for them to ask tough questions about why you are going to do what you propose. They can test your thinking and offer input and personal advice that will improve the overall quality of your plan and approach to improvement.

Your presentation and subsequent discussion with others can have a powerful effect on your motivation, integration, and application—all of which are necessary for real learning and transformation. And when you have two or three people share their improvement plans with each other in this fashion, there is great learning that can take place that can have a real impact on your personal transformation.

Key Coaching Tip #6: Refine and Operationalize Your Plan - Once you've received input from others that you trust on your plan, take the time to revise it as a simple, well-written document that specifies the things that you will Keep Doing, Stop Doing, and Start Doing for the next 90 days. Don't skip this important step of finalizing a plan that you are committed to implementing on a daily basis during the next three months. And remember to keep your plan simple and targeted on the specific things that can have the biggest impact on improving your performance around the 12 Career Success and Survival Imperatives. You are the one who has to live with your plan so make sure that you "own it!"

Key Coaching Tip #7: Share Your 90-Day Action Plan with Your Boss- Now, if you're serious about taking your performance to the next level, you will need to have a serious discussion with your boss to share your plan and make sure that you are both on the same page in terms of the specific results and behaviors that you have identified to improve upon. It is a good strategy to schedule a meeting with your boss, and to also provide them with a written copy of your Personal Performance

Improvement Plan for their review <u>prior</u> to your one-on-one meeting. And depending on the nature of your improvement plan, you may even consider asking for 15 minutes to share your PowerPoint presentation with your boss.

This discussion can send a powerful message to your superior that you are serious about delivering better results and that you have a game plan for doing so. You want to seek out your boss's input on your plan because you are going to need their help during the implementation process. This tip hits home when you ask your boss for 10- to 15-minute performance discussions twice a month for their feedback, coaching, and ongoing alignment and to help you stay on track with your plan. Do not underestimate the importance of pulling your boss into this improvement discussion which sends a powerful message about you while creating an additional layer of accountability for real change. And don't be surprised if your boss seems a little uneasy in this discussion because very few people demonstrate this level of initiative in improving their own performance. But don't worry, most bosses will grow to appreciate your efforts and will be the beneficiaries of your improved performance.

Key Coaching Tip #8: Conduct a Daily S.T.O.P. and Implement the 15/5/5 Rule - Once you have taken the steps to build your plan and create accountability for real change, now it's time to take the most important step that will drive real transformation in your performance. It is imperative for you to develop the habit of conducting daily S.T.O.P.'s—Sit, Think, Optimize, Perform—to create your daily performance scripts that support your specific improvement plan. It is paramount that you learn how to engage in the key activities that will enhance and improve your cumulative performance *one day at a time*.

Develop your daily performance scripts so that you target the appropriate results, activities, working relationships, and allocation of your time/organizational resources so that your tactical activities tie directly into your strategic objectives as a "business unit of one."

Fifteen minutes of planning at the start of each day to establish your daily performance script will be critical to your success. At the midpoint of each work day, take five minutes to adjust and realign what you will be able to achieve with the remainder of your day. This adjustment is critical to create appropriate focus and alignment with the changing demands of each and every day and goes a long way to reduce frustration. And at the end of your day take five additional minutes to conduct a postgame analysis on lessons learned that day and how your plan will roll forward into the next day. Remember what was shared in the book about the 15/5/5 Rule: effectively engaging in this practice can translate into a significant gain in your personal performance and productivity along many dimensions and is the key to behaving with greater intentionality in the workplace.

Key Coaching Tip #9: Conduct a Strategic S.T.O.P. Each Month with Yourself and Your Accountability Partner/Personal Board of Directors to Track Progress - Know that there is no substitute for ongoing focus, self-appraisal, feedback, coaching, and accountability if you are serious about improving your performance. It will behoove you to engage in monthly strategic S.T.O.P.'s to determine your performance against your Personal Performance Improvement Plan. At the same time, conducting three monthly follow-up meetings with your accountability team can be an exceptionally good use of your time. A breakfast meeting or lunch is usually sufficient for a review of your performance against your performance plan and will provide you an opportunity to share your wins, struggles, and frustrations with people who are in a position to encourage you and help you stay on track!

I cannot overemphasize the importance of having an accountability partner or personal board of directors to help you on your journey to be the best you that you can possibly be! And after doing this for three months, you just might find that this is a practice you wish to roll forward for the rest of your career and especially after you learn the benefits of coaching and helping your accountability partner or other members of your board go through the same improvement process themselves!

Key Coaching Tip #10: Never Underestimate the Power of Slowing Down, Unplugging, and Taking Time to THINK - One of the biggest things that I have learned over the course of my career is the power of slowing down, being still, and taking the time to think before I perform. Taking the time to think on a daily, weekly, monthly, quarterly, and yearly basis about what you are trying to accomplish in each of these time frames can have a powerful effect on your ability to deliver the right results, at the right time, in the right way. Know that if you do not plan to slow down and set aside specific times to think and reflect, you will never reach your full potential as a professional/leader. The most powerful weapon you can use in your quest for career success is your ability to think and adjust your behavior to the ever changing demands of your work situation.

A CLOSING THOUGHT: I would like to conclude *The Successful Career Survival Guide* with a powerful quote from the great American humorist, entrepreneur, and author Samuel Langhorne Clemens, whom we know by his pen name Mark Twain: ***"The two most important days in your life are the day you were born and the day you find out why."*** It is my wish that this book might help you better achieve your career aspirations and dreams as you seek to realize the second most important day of your life—the WHY.

APPENDIX

The 12 Career Success and Survival Imperative Questions

Instructions: Answer these specific questions for yourself in your quest to improve your performance and your career trajectory. Your response to these questions will help you identify some of the specific actions that you will need to take to improve your game!

1. What specific things do I need to do to identify and deliver the <u>desired results</u> my organization wants and needs from me on a more consistent basis?

2. What specific things do I need to do to better recognize, implement, and master the <u>practices/behaviors</u> that lead to desired results on an ongoing basis?

3. What specific things do I need to do to better focus my <u>time</u>, <u>organizational resources</u>, and <u>power</u> on delivering desired results?

4. What specific things do I need to do to better forge and maintain viable, effective <u>working relationships</u> and <u>business networks </u>with the people I need to get desired results?

5. What specific things do I need to do to more effectively <u>communicate</u> and <u>connect</u> <u>with</u> everyone in every situation at work?

6. What specific things do I need to do to better maintain and project a positive <u>personality</u>, <u>attitude</u>, and <u>outlook</u> about myself, my work, and my life?

7. What specific things do I need to do to better maintain and expand my "situational awareness" so that I always know what is going on around me and how well I am actually performing?

8. What specific things do I need to do better to learn and develop the skills/talents necessary to meet the changing demands of my job?

9. What specific things do I need to do to better embrace feedback and coaching and create accountability for improvement?

10. What specific things do I need to do to be a more disciplined problem-solver and change agent to make it easier to get things done?

11. What specific things do I need to do to better handle stress, stay poised, and maintain balance in every area of my personal and professional life?

12. What specific things do I need to do to better demonstrate character and integrity in all of my personal and professional dealings?

ABOUT THE AUTHOR

Clinton Oliver Longenecker, PhD, is an award-winning business educator, author, researcher, consultant, and speaker and is one of "America's leaders in creating high-performance leaders and organizations."

He is a Distinguished University Professor and the Director of the Center for Leadership and Organizational Excellence in the College of Business and Innovation at the University of Toledo. His teaching, research, and consulting interests are in high-performance leadership and creating great organizations.

He has been the recipient of over 60 outstanding teaching, service, and research awards and numerous industry awards including the Ernst & Young Entrepreneur of the Year, Toastmasters International Leadership Award, and the Jefferson Award for Outstanding Public Service, as well as numerous "Best Professor" recognitions. In addition, he has also been recently recognized by *The Economist* as one of the Top Fifteen Business Professors in the World. In 2017, Clint was recognized as one of the top three University Professors in the USA as a Finalist for Baylor University's Robert Foster Cherry Award for Great Teaching and as one of the top 30 "transformational leaders" in America by The John Maxwell Organization.

He has published over 200 articles and papers in leading academic and professional journals including the *Sloan Management Review, Strategic HR Review, Industrial Management, Business Horizons, European Business Review,* and *Organizational Dynamics,* among others. He is a frequent media source and his research has been featured in the *Wall Street Journal,* Investor's Business Daily, MSNBC, NPR and a wide variety of media outlets. Clint is also a critically acclaimed professor in the Great Courses: Critical Business Skills for Success series, and a coauthor of two best-selling leadership books, *Getting Results: Five Absolutes for High Performance* and *Two-Minute Drill: Lessons for Rapid Organizational Improvement from America's Greatest Game.*

Clint is an active management consultant, educator, and executive coach whose clients include a wide variety of Fortune 500 firms and entrepreneurial organizations, including Harley-Davidson; Conagra; SSOE Group; ProMedica Health Systems; Whirlpool; Eaton; Cooper Tire; Dana Inc.; Howard Hughes Medical Institute; and O-I,

Inc. among others. Clint has been described by Career Publications as *"one of the top motivational speakers in the US who can blend cutting-edge research, common sense, humor, and conviction into a real and inspiring call for better performance that can help us all!"*

Clint has also served as a visiting lecturer at the University of the West Indies Barbados and has lectured extensively in Poland, Hungary, and Russia. He holds a BBA in marketing, an MBA in management, both from the University of Toledo, and a PhD in management from Pennsylvania State University.

Clint is an active community servant, a committed member of the Christian and Missionary Alliance Church and an active Bible study leader and Christian speaker. He has spent extensive time working in the country of Haiti managing missionary school and hospital construction projects. Clint is very happily married to a wonderful woman named Cindy, and they have three children, Clinton Charles, Shannon Marie, and Stephen Lorenzo.

Connect with Clint
e-mail: clinton.longenecker@utoledo.edu
www.homepages.utoledo.edu/clongen/

References and Additional Readings

Longenecker, C.O., and Fink, L.S., "Serious Lessons for Managing Your Boss in the 21ST Century," *Industrial Management* May/June 2016, pp. 10-15.

Longenecker, C.O., "Why Leaders Fail to Deliver Desired Results," *The Drake Business Review*, Vol. 8 No. 1, 2016, pp. 22-26.

Longenecker, C.O., and Fink, L.S. "U.S. Trends in Formal Performance Appraisal: A Time for Organizational Self-Appraisal," *Journal of Compensation and Benefits*, May/June 2015, pp. 5-12.

Longenecker, C.O., "Career Success: Voices from the Trenches," *Industrial Management,* March/April 2015, pp. 20-25.

Longenecker, C.O., "The Best Practices of Great Leaders," *Industrial Management.* January/February 2015, pp. 20-25.

Longenecker, C.O., Goldsby, T.J., Hamilton, R., Roberto, M.A., and Sussman, E., "Critical Business Skills for Success," The Great Courses, 2015.

Longenecker, C.O. and Longenecker, P.D. "Barrier and Gateways to Healthcare Change," *The Journal of Healthcare Management* Volume 59, No. 2. March/April 2014, pp.147-157.

Longenecker, C.O., "How to Become the Best Leader You Can Be," *The Drake Business Review*, Vol. 6, No. 2, 2014, pp. 7-11.

Longenecker, C.O., Mallin, M., and Ragland, C., "The Sales Manager Development Gap: Are Leaders Equipped to Walk the Walk?" *The Journal of Selling and Major Account Management*, 2014.

Longenecker, C.O., Mallin, M., and Ragland, C., "Developing High Performance Sales Managers: Key Practices for Accelerating Growth," *Development and Learning in Organizations: An International Journal*, Vol. 28, No. 20, 2014, pp.10-13.

Longenecker, C.O. and Fink, L. S. "The Top 10 Reasons That Key Managers Leave," *Human Resource Management International Digest*, Vol. 22, No. 2, 2014, pp. 36-38.

Longenecker, C. O. and Abernathy, R. K., "The Eight Imperatives for Effective Adult Learning". *Human Resource Management International Digest*, Vol. 21, No. 7, 2014, pp. 30-33.

Longenecker, C.O. and Fink, L. S., "Tipping Points for Involuntary Turnover," *Industrial Management*. May/June 2013, pp. 10-15.

Longenecker, C.O., Yonker, R. "Leadership Deficiencies in Rapidly Changing Organizations: Multisource Feedback as a Needs Assessment Tool – Part I." *Industrial and Commercial Training*. Vol. 45, No. 3, 2013, pp. 159-165.

Longenecker, C.O., Yonker, R. "Leadership Deficiencies in Rapidly Changing Organizations: Multisource Feedback as a Needs Assessment Tool – Part II." *Industrial and Commercial Training*. Vol. 45, No. 4, 2013, pp. 202-208.

Longenecker, C.O. Beard, S. and Scazerro, J.A., "What about the Workers? The Workforce Benefits of Corporate Volunteer Programs," *Development and Learning in Organizations: An International Journal*. Vol. 27, No. 1, 2013, pp. 9-13.

Chupp, B., Longenecker, C.O., and Ariss, S.A., "On the Minds of Entrepreneurs: How Entrepreneurs Learn," *Effective Executive Journal*. Vol. XVI, No. 1, 2013, pp. 7-15.

Longenecker, C.O. and Fink, L. S. "The Attributes of Great Human Resource Leaders," *HR Advisor Journal*, December 2012, pp. 5-12.

Longenecker, C.O. and Fink, L. S., "Fixing Management's Fatal Flaws," *Industrial Management*, July/August 2012, pp. 12-17.

Longenecker, C.O. "The Characteristics of Really Bad Bosses," *Industrial Management*, September/October 2011, pp.10-15.

Longenecker, C.O. Moore, G. and Scazerro, J.A., "The Benefits of Corporate Volunteer Programs: An Employee's Perspective," *HR Advisor Journal.* September/October 2011, pp. 6-14.

Longenecker, C.O. and Fink, L. S., "The New HRM Reality: HR Leadership in Trying Economic Times," *HR Advisor Journal.* March/April, 2011.

Longenecker, C.O., "How the Best Motivate Workers," *Industrial Management.* January/February, 2011, pp.8-13.

Longenecker, C.O. "Career Survival and Success in the 21st Century," *Drake Business Review.* Vol. 3, No. 2, 2011, pp. 8-12.

Longenecker, C.O. and Gatins, D. "Gateways to Management Development in Rapidly Changing Organizations," *Development and Learning in Organizations: An International Journal.* Vol.25, No.3. 2011, pp. 3-6.

Longenecker, C.O. "Getting Better Results: Ten Leadership Imperatives," *Drake Business Review.* Winter 2010.

Longenecker, C.O. "Key Practices for Closing the Management Skills Gap," *HRM Review.* May 2010, pp. 19- 25.

Longenecker, C.O., "Barriers to Managerial Learning: Lessons for Rapidly Changing Organizations," *Development and Learning in Organizations: An International Journal.* Vol. 24 No.5. 2010, pp. 8-11.

Longenecker, C.O. "Coaching for Better Results: Key Practices of High Performance Leaders," *Industrial and Commercial Training.* Vol. 42 No.1, 2010. pp. 32-40.

Longenecker, C.O., Papp, G.R., and Stansfield, T.S., "Quarterbacking Real and Rapid Organizational Improvement." *Leader-to-Leader.* Number 51, Winter 2009, pp. 17-23.

Longenecker, C.O. and Ariss, S.S. "Leading in Trying Economic Times: Imperatives for Handling the Heat," *Industrial Management,* September/October 2009. pp. 8- 12.

Fink, L.S. and Longenecker, C.O. "Appraising Managerial Performance in Challenging Economic Times: Part 2," *Journal of Compensation and Benefits*. July/August 2009,
pp. 5-12.

Longenecker, C.O. and Fink, L.S. "Appraising Managerial Performance in Challenging Economic Times: Part 1," *Journal of Compensation and Benefits*. May/June 2009, pp. 6-12.

Longenecker, C.O. Smallman, B.S. and Wang, H. "Managerial Career Success in 21st Century China," *HR International Journal*. Spring 2009, pp. 13-20.

Longenecker, C.O., Yonker, R. and McGoldrick, L. "The Competitive Professional Benefits of Managerial Health," *Development and Learning in Organizations: An International Journal*. Vol. 23, No.5, 2009. pp. 19-21.

Fink, L. S., Longenecker, C.O., and Cutcher, A. "Creating Human Resource Management Value in Challenging Economic Times," *HR Advisor Journal*. May/June 2009, pp. 13-22.

Longenecker, C.O. and Simonetti, J.L. "Staffing for Better Results: Key Practices of High Performance Mangers." *HRM Review*. December 2008, pp. 20-25.

Longenecker, C.O. and Fink, L.S. "Developing a Learning Organization: The Top Management Leadership Factor." *Effective Executive*, June 2008, pp. 46-51.

Stansfield, T.S., Papp, G.R., and Longenecker, C.O., "Effective Manufacturing Improvement," *Industrial Management* January/February 2008, pp. 24-30.

Longenecker, C.O., Papp, G.R., and Stansfield, T.S., "Post Change Analysis: Learning from Change." *Development and Learning in Organizations: An International Journal*. Vol. 22, No. 6, 2008. pp. 11-14.

Longenecker, C.O. and Fink, L.S. "Key Criteria in 21st Century Management Promotional Decisions," *Career Development International*. Vol.13, No. 3, 2008, pp. 241-251.

Longenecker, C.O., Neubert, M.J, and Fink, L.S., "Causes and Consequences of Managerial Failure in Rapidly Changing Organizations," *Business Horizons*, Vol. 50 No. 2, March/April 2007, pp. 145-155.

Longenecker, C.O., Papp, G., and Stansfield, T. *Two-Minute Drill: Lessons for Rapid Organizational Improvement from America's Greatest Game*. Jossey- Bass Publishers; San Francisco, 2007.

Longenecker, C.O. "The Training Practices of Results-Oriented Leaders," *Industrial and Commercial Training*. Vol. 39 No. 7, 2007, pp. 361-367.

Longenecker, C.O. and Rieman, M., "Making Organizational Change Stick: Leadership Reality Checks," *Development and Learning in Organizations: An International Journal*. Vol. 21, No. 5, 2007, pp. 7-10.

Longenecker, C.O., Papp G, and Stansfield T.C., "Characteristics of Successful Improvement Initiatives," *Industrial Management*. September/October 2006, pp. 25-30.

Longenecker, C.O. and Fink L.S., "On Employee Self-Appraisals: Benefits and Opportunities," *Journal of Compensation and Benefits*, May/June 2006, pp. 12-18.

Longenecker, C.O. and Fink, L.S., "How Top Managers Develop: A Field Study," *Organizational Development and Learning: An International Journal*, Vol. 20, No.5, 2006, pp. 18-20.

Stansfield, T.C. and Longenecker, C.O., "The Effects of Goal Setting on Manufacturing Productivity: A Field Experiment," *International Journal of Productivity and Performance Management*, Vol.55 No. 3/4, 2006, pp. 346- 358.

Longenecker, C.O. and Fink, L.S., "Closing the Management Skills Gap: A Call for Action," *Development and Learning in Organizations: An International Journal*, Vol. 20, No.1, 2006, pp. 16-20.

Longenecker, C.O. and Ariss, S.S., "Why Service Organizations Fail to get Desired Results: The Front-Line Manager's Perspective," *International Journal of Effective Management*, Vol. 2, No. 1, 2005, pp. 1-17.

Longenecker, C.O. and Neubert, M.J., "The Practices of Effective Managerial Coaches: Voices from the Field," *Business Horizons*, Volume 48, 2005, pp. 493-500.

Longenecker, C.O. and Simonetti, J.L. "The Call for Results," *Management Skills: A Jossey-Bass Reader*. Jossey-Bass Publishers; San Francisco, 2005, pp. 477- 487.

Longenecker, C.O. and Ariss, S.S. "Who Goes and Who Stays: Managerial Criteria for Downsizing Decisions," *Industrial Management*, 2004. May-June 2004, pp. 8-15. *Development and Learning: An International*. Vol. 18, No. 4, 2004, pp 3-6.

Neubert, M.J. and Longenecker, C.O., "Creating Job Clarity: HR's Role in Creating Organizational Focus," *The HR Advisor Journal*, June/July 2003, pp.17-24.

Stansfield, T.C. and Longenecker, C.O., "Solidifying Startup Success," *Industrial Management*, March/April 2003, pp.24-30.

Longenecker, C.O. and Neubert, M.J., "The Management Development Needs of Front-Line Managers: Voices from the Field," *Career Development International*, Volume 8, Issue 4, 2003, pp. 210-218.

Longenecker, C.O. and Scazzero, J.A., "Turnover and Retention of IT Managers in Rapidly Changing Organizations," *Information Systems Management*, 2003, pp. 58-63.

Longenecker, C.O. and Leffakis, Z. M., Serious about White Collar Productivity," *Industrial Management*, November/December 2002 pp. 27-33.

Longenecker, C.O. and Ariss, S.S., "Creating Competitive Advantage Through Effective Management Education," *Journal of Management Development*, Vol. 21, No. 9, 2002, pp. 640-654.

Longenecker, C.O. and Gioia, D.A., "Confronting the Politics in Performance Appraisal," *Business Forum*, 2002 Vol. 25, No. 3, 2001 pp. 17-23.

Longenecker, C.O. "Building High Performance Management Teams," *Industrial Management*, November-December, 2001, pp. 21-26.

Longenecker, C.O. and Simonetti, J.L. *Getting Results: Five Absolutes for High Performance*. The University of Michigan Business School Book Series, Jossey-Bass Publishers; San Francisco, 2001.

Longenecker, C.O. and Fink, L.S. "Improving Management Performance in Rapidly Changing Organizations," *Journal of Management Development*, Vol. 20, No.1, 2001, pp. 336-46.

Longenecker, C.O. and Neubert, M. "Barriers and Gateways to Management Cooperation and Teamwork," *Business Horizons*, September-October 2000, pp. 37-44.

Longenecker, C.O. and Stansfield, T.C. "Why Plant Managers Fail: Causes and Consequences," *Industrial Management* January-February 2000, pp. 24-32.

Longenecker, C.O. and Scazzero, J.A. "Improving Service Quality: A Tale of Two Operations," *Managing Service Quality*, Vol. 10, No. 4, 2000, pp. 227-232.

Longenecker, C.O., Schaffer, C.J. and Scazzero, J.A. "Under the Gun: Causes and Consequences of Stress in the Information Technology Profession," *Information Systems Management*, Summer 1999, pp. 71-77.

Longenecker, C.O., Simonetti, S.L. and Sharkey, T.W. "Why Organizations Fail: The View from the Front-Line," *Management Decision Journal*, Vol. 37, No. 6, 1999, pp. 503-513.

Longenecker, C.O. and Dwyer, D.J. "The Role of Human Resource Management in Creating Competitive Advantage," *The HR Advisor Journal*, March-April, 1998 pp. 5-12.

Longenecker, C.O., Dwyer, D.J. and Stansfield, T.C. "Barriers and Gateways to Workforce Productivity: Lessons to be Learned," *Industrial Management*, April-March, pp. 21-28.

Longenecker, C.O., Simonetti, J.L. and LaHote D. "Increasing the ROI on Management Education Efforts," *Career Development International*, 1998, Vol. 3, No. 4, pp. 154-160.

Longenecker, C.O. "The Consequences and Causes of Ineffective Organizational Training Practices," *The HR Advisor*, November-December 1997, pp. 5-13.

Longenecker, C.O., Simonetti, J.L., Nykodym, N. and Scazzero, J.A. "Thinning The Herd: Twelve Factors Affecting Downsizing Decisions," *The H.R. Advisor Journal*, March-April 1997, pp. 16-22.

Longenecker, C.O. and Pinkel, P. "Coaching to Win at Work," *Manage*, January-February 1997, pp. 19-21.

Longenecker, C.O., Stansfield, T.C., and Dwyer, D.J. "The Human Side of Manufacturing Improvement," *Business Horizon*, March-April 1997, pp. 7-17.

Longenecker, C.O. and Meade, W.D. "Marketing as a Management Style," *Business Horizons*, July-August 1995, pp. 77-83.

Longenecker, C.O. and Gioia, D.A. "The Politics of Executive Appraisal," *Journal of Compensation and Benefits*, September-October 1994, pp. 5-11.

Longenecker, C.O. and Post, F. "The Management Termination Trap," *Business Horizons*, May-June 1994, pp. 30-40.

Longenecker, C.O., Scazzero, J.A., and Stansfield, T.T. "Quality Improvement Through Team Goal Setting, Feedback, and Problem Solving: A Field Experiment," *International Journal of Quality and Reliability Management*, Vol. 7, No. 3, 1994, pp. 45-52.

Ludwig, D.C. and Longenecker, C.O. "The Bathsheba Syndrome: The Ethical Failures of Successful Leaders," *Journal of Business Ethics*, Vol. 12, 1993, pp. 265-273.

Longenecker, C.O. and Scazzero, J.A. "Creating a Climate for Quality," *Supervision*, January 1993, pp. 14-16.

Longenecker, C.O. and Gioia, D.A. "The Myth of Managing Managers," *The Sloan Management Review*, Fall 1991, pp. 51-60.

Longenecker, C.O. and Ludwig, D.C. "Ethical Dilemmas in Performance Appraisal Revisited," *The Journal of Business Ethics*, Number 9, 1990, pp. 53-61.

Longenecker, C.O. "Truth or Consequences: Politics and Performance Appraisal," *Business Horizons*, Nov-Dec 1989, pp. 76-82.

Author's Note: A special thank you to the thousands of the leaders and professionals who have participated in our ongoing applied research studies over the years! Thank you for sharing your priceless ideas, perceptions, opinions, and best practices!